FATHER
GOD

Other Books by Sylvia Browne

Adventures of a Psychic (with Antoinette May)
Astrology Through a Psychic's Eyes
Blessings from the Other Side (with Lindsay Harrison)
Contacting Your Spirit Guide (book-with-CD)
Conversations with the Other Side
Exploring the Levels of Creation
The Healing Journey (available February 2008)
If You Could See What I See
A Journal of Love and Healing (with Nancy Dufresne)
Life on the Other Side (with Lindsay Harrison)
Meditations
Mother God
The Other Side and Back (with Lindsay Harrison)
Past Lives, Future Healing (with Lindsay Harrison)
Prayers
Prophecy (with Lindsay Harrison)
Secrets & Mysteries of the World
Secret Societies (available September 2007)
Sylvia Browne's Book of Angels
Sylvia Browne's Book of Dreams (with Lindsay Harrison)
Sylvia Browne's Lessons for Life
Visits from the Afterlife (with Lindsay Harrison)

The Journey of the Soul Series
(available individually or in a boxed set)

God, Creation, and Tools for Life (Book 1)
Soul's Perfection (Book 2)
The Nature of Good and Evil (Book 3)

FATHER
GOD

CO-CREATOR
TO MOTHER GOD

SYLVIA BROWNE

HAY HOUSE, INC.
Carlsbad, California
London • Sydney • Johannesburg
Vancouver • Hong Kong • New Delhi

Copyright © 2007 by Sylvia Browne

Editorial supervision: Jill Kramer • *Design:* Suzie Bergstrom

All rights reserved. No part of this book may be reproduced by any mechanical, photographic, or electronic process, or in the form of a phonographic recording; nor may it be stored in a retrieval system, transmitted, or otherwise be copied for public or private use—other than for "fair use" as brief quotations embodied in articles and reviews—without prior written permission of the publisher. The intent of the author is only to offer information of a general nature to help you in your quest for emotional and spiritual well-being. In the event you use any of the information in this book for yourself, which is your constitutional right, the author and the publisher assume no responsibility for your actions.

ISBN: 978-1-4019-0533-0

Printed in the United States of America

To my grandchildren:
Willy, Angelia, and Jeff

CONTENTS

INTRODUCTION

The 50-plus years of research that I've done have enabled me to accumulate an amazing amount of knowledge about our Father God. I've studied the subject for decades, as well as receiving information from my spirit guide Francine. (For those of you who don't know about Francine, she's been guiding me since the very beginning of my journey in this lifetime. She's a great researcher and has been proven right over and over again—even things that seemed preposterous at the time have been found to be true over the years.)

Since I've previously written about Mother God, it's only logical that I'd share what I know about our Father with the world. I won't be having any conversations with our beloved Creator in this book; rather, the information I'll give you in these pages has been garnered from years of research.

Don't get me wrong, though—I talk to God all the time and feel His presence (as I do our Mother's) all around me and get signs that He keeps us forever in His hands. We can all hear God in our souls if we're just quiet enough to listen.

In fact, those whom we call "primitive" had a much better or closer relationship with God. The God (or gods) of the Africans, Aborigines, Polynesians, Incans, Aztecs, and Egyptians was very personal. As we've become more . . . not civilized, but I think *un*civilized . . . we've lost God. We've stated that He cared, then He didn't care, then He abandoned us, and then He was dead.

It's often hard for us to look at the atrocities in this world and simply accept that there is a loving God. Wars, children dying, abject poverty, pestilence, molestations, murders, human-rights violations, bigotry, and human beings' general cruelty to each other are events that we hear or read about every day— and many of us can't understand that above all this horror stands a loving God. So many of us choose to either not believe in Him anymore or just ignore the whole concept altogether.

It's perfectly natural (because we *are* human, of course) to get mad at God, but then most of us feel guilty about it or think that we've lost our faith. With the holy books of the Bible, the Qur'an (also known as the Koran), *The Egyptian Book of the Dead,* and the Talmud, along with the tomes of theologians and writers from every religion, it's no wonder that we're confused. And yes, I fit into this category, too, so I can only give you what I know to be an uncomplicated, simplistic truth without any trimmings. I'd also like to repeat, as I tend to do in my books, that you should take with you what you want and leave the rest.

Many people have told me that they always believed what I put forward in my works, but they were afraid to speak it themselves. Why? Well, because of religious dogma (human-made, I might add) or because these individuals feel that others wouldn't find them "mainstream" or within the so-called acceptable norm of belonging to one of the world's religions.

Going through all the related transcripts in my company's archives, as well as over my own knowledge of the subject, was no small feat. I'm not complaining, because what better glorious subject to explore than our Creator? And even as Francine says, with as much information as we can collect, it's only a thumbnail sketch compared to the continuous quest for God that we forever pursue on the Other Side after we pass over. I hope you will enjoy this book, which is my take on the Father Who loves us all.

~~ ~~ ~~ ~~ ~~

Chapter One

THE HISTORY OF
FATHER GOD

The first thing we should address, which my clients and readers ask me about all the time, is whether or not God is a real entity. From what my guide Francine has told me (she knows firsthand, as all of us do when we go to the Other Side), the answer is yes. However, she added that unlike Azna, our Mother God, He doesn't hold His form for too long.

I was talking to my son about this one night, and he wondered, "But Mom, if He's God, then why doesn't He hold His form?"

Damn . . . back to the drawing board. When I asked Francine about this, she said, "Of course He could hold a shape forever if He chose to, but He chooses to stay in spirit form because that way He can be, as we might say, spread out everywhere." Azna the Mother God is the same, but she's more active and can take a form easier and more frequently.

It's interesting to note that when we've all seen Him on the Other Side, He has what we can imagine as a Christlike figure (or at least how artists usually depict him). I don't mean to confuse the two or say that Jesus was God—and I'd certainly never discredit Jesus— but I sometimes wonder if, when people think that they're seeing a Christ figure, they're actually seeing our Father. He stands very tall and usually comes with this blinding light that then tones down from silver to gold to purple. He has beautiful, handsome features and has come in both dark and light coloring, even at times appearing Hispanic, Indian, or Asian—but you always know Him by His stately stance. He is a tall, angular figure with beautiful hands and enormous eyes . . . and He has never appeared as an old man with a beard.

So God *does* have a real "physical" form. The problem is that He, unlike Mother God, chooses not to hold it for long because His magnificent strength of being is so strong that to confine it to a singular image or form is almost contradictory to His nature of being all-encompassing and an integral part of the makeup of every creation.

Our Mother doesn't have the controversial history that our Father does. As I stated in my book *Mother God,* although She surfaces throughout history, She has been submerged, as Her temples and the writings about Her were destroyed. Yet strangely enough, God the Father can be more contradictory and confusing than She is. The reason for this, of course, is because we've been under the patriarchal rule for so long, while She has been kept buried for 2,000 years. So when someone such as a true deity (Mother God) has been submerged, it's harder to refute or dispute except from just pure logic.

If any one being besides Jesus has been judged so horribly, it's our Mother and Father both . . . one was almost annihilated, and the other became an unforgiving monster. It's much like Mel Gibson's movie *The Passion of the Christ*—to make it even *seem* anti-Semitic was ludicrous. Mr. Gibson took a small band of politically motivated people who were ruled by the Romans, and he blamed Christ's death on them. Need we go back to the Holy Inquisition or revisit the other atrocities perpetrated in the name of Christianity? Religion is run by men, while spiritual works and deeds are just that. You can't blame the whole for the actions of a few, the same as you can't accuse every priest of being a pedophile or fault all of Islam for the actions of a handful of terrorists.

Our Father has many names, just as our Mother has. He's been called "Yahweh," "Jehovah," "Allah," "Om," and "God," as well as many more. Theologians tell us that His true name is sacred and no one can know it, thus making Him very picky and humanized, which I've always tried to dispel. As He states in the Old Testament: "I am Who I am." It doesn't matter what you call God because He is all things to everyone, so whatever makes you comfortable is fine.

I remember a young boy coming up to me after a lecture in Egypt, asking if God minded being called Allah. "Of course not," I replied. "He could answer to George." What's in a name? After all, it's all the same deity. My nickname is Syl, but when I lived in Missouri I was known as Sylvi or Sissy. Does this make me different? No, it doesn't—I'm the same entity no matter what you call me.

❧ ❧ ❧

Coming from what I like to call "the Divine Sparkler," we're each sparks of the creative force of Father and Mother God. You see, if we have two sides to our brain, male and female, it's the same with the mirror of creation. Our solid, static Father is the co-creator and is all intellect, while our Mother is the emotional, active, and we could say "interfering" God Who makes miracles in our charts (the "blueprint" that each of us chooses and designs for every life we live). We needed to have the intellect to pick our charts, but most feeling was left out—after all, if all the emotion in life seeped in, we might not be so inclined to go back to Earth for another round. God the Father helps us mold our charts to learn not only intellectually what we must go through for our own soul's perfection, but also to feed data back to Him.

While knowledge is one facet of life on Earth, emotion is the other, and even if God knows everything, we still live for Him. The communion we share with our Father is part of the greatest love affair that will ever be.

Now the reason that God was made so ominous was that humankind's emerging religions had to make their deity more ferocious and powerful than those that had existed before. It was almost like the sentiment of "my dad can beat up your dad." Most religions will say that He created everything (including human beings) in a time frame, but that's impossible for our Father. It would mean that one day He decided He was lonely or bored or even wanted someone to worship Him. God is always in the now (the concept of no time or no passage of time), perfect, all-knowing, and all-loving. Deciding to make something is again giving Him human traits.

I think this is why Buddhists can't understand our concept of God because He has so many religious contradictions, especially in the Bible. It's even understandable why Christians have a hard time with the God of the Old Testament Who, on a whim, brought plague, famine, and destruction to the very people He supposedly loved. (I explain more about the world's religions in Chapters 2 and 3.)

The logic of the contradictory God of organized monotheistic religion seems to elude humankind—we dutifully wade through the dogma of the various major faiths, despite the fact that the love of God and doing good is so simple! We're not sent down to toil in the fields, as Genesis states. If we're not to gain knowledge from an all-loving God Who loves us equally, then what's the point of going through life with its hardships and pain?

It makes perfect sense that we're here to advance for ourselves and learn for our souls and our beloved God. As I've already stated, we write out our charts to experience for God and ascend to a higher place of knowledge, and this is something we can all attain through many lifetimes. Life is a school, and each level brings us different experiences so that our soul grows

. . . otherwise, we're left with a God Who plays chess with our existences.

Do I believe that down here on the Earth plane we depend on God? Of course I do! Even with the chart that we've written, we sometimes bite off more than we can chew, so we put our hand in His to pull us out of the quicksand of life. Although our charts are written in advance, our Mother and Father don't turn a blind eye to our plight. It's like they're saying, "If you come to Us, We will heal your wounds and make them bearable. While We may have given you the free will to progress, We have never abandoned you."

Those of us who are parents have watched our children make mistakes and sometimes go through life the hard way. Even as we try to give them comfort and solace, we also know that they have to learn. We might not be able to prevent the scrapes and bruises, but we can certainly hold our kids and put salve on their wounds . . . and so do Mother and Father God. We don't always see Their help at the time—not until after the pain has subsided do we realize that everything truly does happen for the best. This includes death, because we and our loved ones reunite and can bask in the glory that is God.

Before we further explore what our Father can do, let's look at His origins in human history.

Our Always-Loving Creator

I find it interesting that the earlier we go to what religious writings or history call "pagan" times, the more loving the god(s). Could this be because politics and money hadn't entered into the picture yet? Yes, there was a fair amount of fear during those times, but it doesn't come anywhere close to what we've heard from the theologians over the past 2,000 years.

Dagda

When I went back to research the Celtic Father God, I almost fell over. How could I have missed this? You see, years ago in a trance session with Francine, someone asked her what God's real name was. Without hesitation, she said, "Dowra." Now most of us have heard of Yahweh, Jehovah, God, or Allah . . . but not Dowra. At the time, I let it sink in but never paid that much attention (I like to refer to Him as Om).

Well, while visiting the Website **www.paganism. com,** I came across an article that referred to God as "Dagda." While it's not the same as Dowra, it's certainly closer than the other so-called names of God are. This God of the Celts seems likely to have been adopted by the early Christian community in the area, perhaps because He was omniscient and seemed to be a good paternal figure. He also had many characteristics attributed to Him, whereas most other ancient deities were only relegated to wind or storms or fertility. The two belief systems of Celtic paganism and early Christianity seem to drift toward each other and became somewhat welded together.

The difference for the Celts is that there was nothing separating the Divine from the secular; in other words, everyday actions could be sacred. They had their godly archetypes (much like our spirit guides or angels) residing in the "Otherworld" or Other Side, and they hoped to learn things such as honor, bravery, and reverence for all of nature. The Celts expressed their hopes, dreams, and aspirations to Dagda and hoped that He would make them eternal.

When the people became Christian, they made sure that their beliefs blended with the new Christian faith. Among the main influences of Celtic Christianity, the first and greatest was that of the Druids—of whom Dagda was a patron god. The Druids and the Celts incorporated many of their concepts, symbols, and ceremonies into Christianity. For example, Dagda had a daughter named Bridget who was a goddess, and she was eventually embraced by Christianity as a saint. (I guess if you can't beat 'em, join 'em or absorb 'em.)

Dagda means "the good god," and he made the seasons change and ensured that everyone was satisfied. He was also referred to as "Eochaid Ollathiar" or "Eochaid, the Father of All," and He denoted fertility. Stories of His union with the goddess Morrigan brought forth the concept of Mother Earth joining with Father Sky. Many used this story as a time to share in a festival for fruitfulness.

El

Next we come to the religion of the Canaanites. Here, God was known as "El," which became the "generic name" for God for many years. The Website **www.northernway.org** says that El was the head of the pantheon of Canaanite paganism and was a shadowy figure at that time. Since He wasn't viewed as pleasant, I feel that He may be thought of as a primitive deity, even more so than the Celtic Dagda.

Although El was given to creating enemies and sordid escapades, the site goes on to say that "we should not be dismayed by the 'bad things' the Canaanite version of El was said to have done. Canaanite and Phoenician society was supposedly depraved (child sacrifice, sex slavery, vicious torture), and so they made their gods and goddesses as violent and as perverse as *them*." Here again we have humans making God imitate *them* instead of leaving Him as He is—perfect in every way.

As time goes on, the true El seems to become one with the Hebrew God; in fact, He is thought to be a part of Yahweh. (Here's another example of a deity being segmented into different parts, much like the Christian Holy Trinity.) El becomes a noble, fatherly, and kindly figure, worshiped not only by the Hebrews in their early days, but also by the desert tribes before the advent of the Islamic religion. In addition, He was the God Who inhabited the sacred mountain areas in the early part of the Old Testament.

In fact, El was the God of the Hebrews even to the time of Moses, and He was referred to as the "God on High." El was thought to be so powerful that He couldn't usually be reached except through a mediator or intermediary, which in the ancient Hebrew tradition would have been an angel. El was thought to be a wise and powerful old man with a white beard, and He sat on top of His throne on a mountaintop between two rivers that fed all the oceans. This type of description still has somewhat of an archetypical influence on our conception of God today.

Bile/Bel

Moving on to Bile (or Bel as He is sometimes called), this is one of the oldest deities with many counterparts in other cultures. Bile is the God of the Underworld, much like his Egyptian counterpart, Anubis. He was also thought to be the husband of Danu, the female complement of this ancient Celtic Divine Being. While he's the Irish father-god of light, healing, and the Otherworld, historians aren't sure if he's Irish in origin because his tradition goes back so far that history blurs.

Named by some writings as "the Father of Gods and Men," Bile is sometimes also called "Balin," "Balar," "Be'al," "Beal," "Beil," and on and on it goes. I bring this pagan god up because he may very well be an offshoot of the infamous Baal of the Bible—and while Bile was considered a great and powerful god by the ancient Celts, the Bible portrays Baal as the epitome of evil.

Baal was the Babylonian and Canaanite ruler of fertility and storms. He also became the God of Human Sacrifice, and historians tell us that many a firstborn was sacrificed to Him to ensure fertility. Some studies say that offerings to Baal were the direct forerunners of human sacrifice in the ancient Hebrew culture, and that He (along with El) was principally worshiped by the Canaanites. We can then make the logical leap that the Old Testament condoned human sacrifice—otherwise, why would God ask Abraham to take his son to the mountain and kill him?

When you get to the core of sacrifice, we can see that primitive humans didn't understand God, so they'd try to appease this force. In other words, sacrifice was born out of fear—give the deity (or deities) your virgins, your grain, your firstborn, your goats, or your fruit. This wasn't symbolism; it was done in actuality. Compare this to the Catholic mass, where eating the body and drinking the blood of Christ are done in emulation. Even cannibalistic cultures believed that if you ate or drank of your enemy, you'd gain the positive attributes that they had.

Historically, from the Greek gods on Mount Olympus or their Roman counterparts on, the deities were always given to human needs and capriciously used us, their subjects, to their own advantage. Anger the gods and you were in for some real trouble. The early Romans and Greeks were afraid to upset them, feeling that their fates were sealed by whether the gods' love and favor fell upon them. Even Genghis Khan, for as much of a barbarian as he was, felt that he was a messenger from God who was in His favor.

It seems no matter how far back you go, people have tried to appease a God Who needed sacrifice or placation in some way in order to bestow His favor upon the group that was the most dutiful to Him.

Trying to Find God

What's fascinating about these ancient stories is that, for the most part, God does seem to be benevolent, self-contained, and part of humankind—not just a voice in a burning bush. It seems that until Christianity took a solid hold, God was more a companion to human beings. Then as religion took hold, He got farther away and harder to reach, and He started playing favorites. We almost have to come to the conclusion that love and harmony don't make money, and they certainly don't ensure control.

We may think that religion was much less difficult in those long-ago times, but it wasn't. Spirituality has always been easy because it's an individual search, but religion has never been that way. Religion and societies grew and marched into what we may jokingly call civilization, but only the best, strongest, and most frightening deity won. Instead of God existing in the very fiber of our being and living in our bodily temple, He was moved outside, and humans made Him into a business.

Most religions believe that where their hallowed ground or edifices of worship are, so resides the "axis mundi" of the world—the sanctified location where all life supposedly revolves, be it the Vatican, Jerusalem, or Mecca. It's wonderful to have a place where the faithful come, but can't God be everywhere? If it accentuates our belief, gives us peace, and helps our love of God become more enhanced, that's great . . . but what if we can't make it to an axis mundi? Well, I assure you that God is with you in every aspect of your life as well as residing inside of you.

This takes us to places of worship. In ancient and biblical times, humans weren't required to have a special day to devote to God. Yes, they had their holy and feast days, and of course they were told to rest on the Sabbath, but we don't hear of Moses building a temple in the desert. He was too busy wandering around trying to find the promised land.

Now while it's true that every culture has had its sacred totems, its blessed mountains or streams, or even its multiple deities of the elements, not until the Sanhedrin (the supreme Jewish legislative and judicial court in Jerusalem during Roman times) began to build temples do we see that there were special days that were set aside for going to a certain place to worship. Early Greeks, Romans, and Egyptians had their temples, but people wandered in and out with petitions to

Zeus or Isis or whoever happened to be the god of a particular temple at that time. As civilization grew, however, people were told that they must attend on either Saturday or Sunday, that they needed to donate money, and that God dwelled within those walls.

What's illogical is that Christ, Buddha, Mohammed, and the like didn't have places of worship. They didn't have glass cathedrals or expensive gold chalices; instead, they walked and talked among the people. It makes you wonder how far afield we got from the simple teachings of these prophets and messengers that came to infuse human beings with hope and love.

It's almost as if humankind has tried to place God in some area where we could find Him, whether it was a burning bush, a mountain or desert, or high on an Aztec pyramid. Thus, out of this need came churches, temples, mosques, and the like. At least people felt that "now we have Him." I don't know about you, but I feel that God being God would be everywhere and with everyone . . . all-seeing and all-knowing and unable to be trapped in any structure. Yet if people feel better in a place of worship, then I think it's wonderful. I've always liked to visit one of them when it's quiet and not many people are present, but I also have a small altar in my bedroom and feel very quiet and close to God there.

Now I'm not trying to be judgmental or critical of

any beliefs. I just want you to travel with me through the long, sometimes confusing, opposing, and humanized edicts and writings about our Creator. I've read some of the works of St. Thomas Aquinas and found them so laborious and often confounding that I just gave up. St. Augustine had some good ideas, but then he resorted to writing about how putrid and sin-filled humans were. Considering the life he led prior to his writings, it's amazing that when he got older, he decided that he knew what sin was.

As we go through all the different writings and then see what a great messenger like Jesus had to say, we find a great divide on what's been said and what's been interpreted. Christ said that if we were like children we would understand. How poignant that is . . . a child scripts truth without guile, while so-called grown-ups add a bunch of words that seem to lend themselves to their own egos rather than simple truth.

An old nun once told me when I started teaching at age 19 that simple is better, and God certainly knows that's true. People get drunk on their own words, and the more complicated and obtuse they are, the more we're supposed to believe that they're filled with the higher intelligence that we stupid mortals can't understand.

Most of the spiritual writings in the Bible, as well as other tomes, have been interpreted, written, and rewritten according to the times and how it all fit into control of the masses. It seems that in this world there's been a very negative factor that virtually instructs: IF YOU ONLY GIVE OUT LOVE AND GOODNESS, NO ONE WILL BELIEVE YOU—AND EVEN MORE IMPORTANT, YOU WON'T SCARE PEOPLE ENOUGH TO EITHER PROPAGATE TO GET MORE MEMBERS OR GIVE MONEY SO THAT YOU CAN BUILD A BIGGER CHURCH.

⁓☙⁓ ⁓☙⁓ ⁓☙⁓

As you read on, please note that there's absolutely no hidden agenda here to make one particular belief lesser or higher than another. Hopefully, you'll research for yourself and see how humankind has muddied up the truth and put it in its own context.

There's an old expression that if you meet Buddha on the road, you should kill him because it wouldn't be the real one. Well, we could say this about the God Whom humans have created—if you meet Him on the road, kill off the false mantles of fear, guilt, and destruction because they snuff out the life of spiritual growth. How much more good can we do knowing that God is kind, loving, and merciful; and that He's always in a state of knowing our hearts, minds, and souls? Life is full of mistakes that we eventually learn from, and this makes us stronger, more spiritual, and more knowledgeable . . . and less apt to repeat our blunders.

Recently I was watching an interview with Billy Graham (who I think is a great man—kind and loving), and he was asked what he'd like to hear our Father say to him when he finally passed over. He thought for a moment and then said, "I think that he's going to say, 'Well done, our good and faithful servant.' Or he may say, 'You're in the wrong place.'"

I was so sad—and even mad—that this wonderful person, who has given his life to "save" people the way he felt was best, would have *any* doubts that an all-loving God would welcome him (as He does all of us) with loving, open arms. If we can use Jesus's parable of the prodigal son, who after many misdeeds comes home to the forgiveness of his human father, then how on Earth could an omnipotent Being do less?

Our Father Is Forever on Our Side

It hurts me that out of 20 or so readings every day, I'll get at least five or six people who are absolutely convinced that God hates them or has abandoned them. They can't help it, as they've been conditioned by years of fear of hellfire, sin, and an unforgiving God. I just tell them, "How could a loving God hate you, especially when you wrote your chart to learn for Him?" Again, we don't give our Father the same failings that we humans have down here on Earth.

(As an aside, I'm reminded of when I tell clients that their loved ones made it to heaven, and they invariably ask me if their friends or family members are happy. Well, of course they are, or it wouldn't be heaven!)

Even though Mother God has long been buried and is rising again, I personally feel that because our Father has been in the forefront for so long, He's actually taken more blows and even been more misunderstood than She has. That's because there has been so much more written about Him—lots of words (with no logic behind them) portraying Him as far away, distant, up in the sky, and unreachable . . . and at the slightest transgression, He can punish us, take our children, send pestilence upon us, curse us, and abandon us. The atrocities that have been written about God are mammoth. It has always been humans' way to try to understand the heinousness of this world, never for a minute wanting to blame their own chart or themselves, or accepting that they could possibly just be here to learn for Him.

Yet at the same time we keep the belief that we have this loving, forgiving Creator. It seems that this sentiment comes to the forefront and is allowable at the time of death, but certainly not through life unless your sins are absolved in some way. (Interestingly, in the Aramaic view of sin, it was seen as nothing more than missing your mark.)

I agree with some of the writings in *The Urantia Book,* especially this: "First and last eternally—the infinite God is a Father in the highest, most perfect sense of that term. He is eternally motivated by the perfect idealism of Divine love and finds its strongest and Divine perfection in loving and being loved. . . . " Now no one knows who wrote this book, but it seems to have come from a collection of people who were infused. The part of God that came to them is the same one that I've been told about, have witnessed, and have researched through death and dying, astral travel, dreams, and a number of past-life regressions that have held up the truth of what Francine has said about our Parents.

God loves like a father—totally selfless and forever in the state of perfect love. Not only are all actions known, but from the lowest creature to the highest, all is centered and created completely in the universal good and perfection of God. Whether it's seasons, storms, life, or death, all are known and part of a Divine plan that at times can seem like chaos, but there is always calm and order . . . and so it is with our loving Father.

This may seem a little laborious, but I'm going to list a few references that are the loving ones in the Bible, which contradicts what you'll find elsewhere about the God of Abraham, Who is far from being loving and perfect:

- God Who gives eternal life (John 12:50)

- God Who has glory (Isaiah 40:5)

- God Who is eternal (Genesis 21:33)

- God Who is in charge of the angels (Psalm 103:20)

- God Who is omnipotent (Matthew 18:19)

- God Who is perfect (Deuteronomy 32:4)

On and on it goes . . . but then you get the God of destruction, who destroyed the Ammonites and Sodom and Gomorrah. In all fairness, we have to view these as stories to scare humankind and keep them on the path of the monotheistic God. Even though I'm convinced that with all of our reason and logic, human beings simply can't reconcile the two, we have a perfect, loving God—and that's the end of it.

~~ ~~ ~~ ~~ ~~

Chapter Two

THE MONOTHEISTIC "BIG THREE"

Judaism, Christianity, and Islam are the "big three" monotheistic religions in the sense that they have the greatest number of followers. Each claims that this "one" God has acted prominently in our theological history—and continues to do so today.

These three religions have scriptures and holy books telling about God, and they have a history that has been joined together constantly. Judaism says that God delivered His people from slavery. Christianity believes in the incarnation of the "savior" and "son of God," Jesus Christ, who died for our sins and was resurrected (the details vary, depending upon what is more emphasized by a particular segment of the faith). Islam speaks of the revelations that God gave the prophet Mohammed through the angel Gabriel.

Notice that all of the big three have a God of salvation in common—and who's to say that their God isn't the right One? Disregarding dogma, the basics of the three seem to be similar, and their history is certainly intermingled. The faiths of Judaism and Islam, for instance, have a strictly one-God concept and can't understand or accept the Holy Trinity of Father, Son, and Holy Spirit adopted by Christianity. In the Qur'an, the concept of three gods is even considered a blasphemy against Allah. By the same token, Christianity can't fathom why others don't accept Christ as a savior . . . so, out of such differences countless wars and inhumanities have taken place.

I'd now like to take the opportunity to explore each of the big three in detail.

Islam

First we have the fast-growing faith of Islam. After 9/11, some individuals have become very prejudiced against Islam, but this is wrong . . . just as it would be wrong to blame all of Christianity for the burning of countless individuals as witches or heretics during the Inquisition. All religions are made up of people, the vast majority of whom are good, honest, and open; and spirituality is a by-product of love that transcends their petty differences and realizes that everyone has their own way of finding God.

Muslims believe that God created the world and then human beings. The first man's name was Adam, whose bloodline led to Noah and his son Shem. Like the Jews, Arabs (the vast majority of whom are Muslim) consider themselves Semitic people—in fact, the word *Semitic* comes from Shem. The descendants of Shem led to Abraham, who was married to Sarah. Sarah was barren, so Abraham took a second wife, Hagar, who bore him a son named Ishmael. Sarah then had a son named Isaac and demanded that Abraham banish Hagar and Ishmael from the tribe, which he did.

Up to this point, both the Bible and the Qur'an agree, except that Islam always calls God "Allah." The Qur'an states that Ishmael went to the place where Mecca (the holy city of Islam) was to rise, and his descendants became Arabs—who eventually became Muslims—while Isaac's offspring eventually became the Jewish people. Notice that the Judaic, Christian, and Islamic religions agree up to this point, after which they become divergent.

Part of this difference stems from the Islamic belief

that the Qur'an (the Holy Scriptures of Islam that were delivered by the prophet Mohammed) is an extension of God's word from the Old and New Testaments of the Bible. The Qur'an was given to Mohammed over the course of 23 years by voices that eventually became one, which identified itself as the angel Gabriel. Evidently Mohammed had no control over the flow of the revelations that descended upon him, so they were written down by his followers.

Muslims believe that there had been authentic messengers of God before Mohammed (such as Jesus, who is considered a great prophet by Islam), but that he was the culmination. He's called "the Seal of the Prophets" by Muslims and supposedly no valid messengers will follow him. According to them, the Qur'an is not only an extension of the Bible, but it's also the final and infallible revelation of God's will.

Followers of Islam believe the Bible to have two defects: (1) It contains only portions of the truth, namely for circumstantial reasons, and (2) it was partially corrupted in transmission. Conversely, they believe the Qur'an to be infallible, which accounts for the occasional discrepancy that occurs between the two books when describing parallel accounts of the same incident. As the second chapter, or *surah,* of the Qur'an explicitly states: "This is the Scripture whereof there is no doubt."

Nevertheless, most scholars say that the Qur'an is one of the most difficult books to read, partly because it was written in Arabic and the translation to other languages doesn't impart the feeling of that language. Although only about 80 percent of the length of the New Testament, most non-Arabic readers find it very esoteric, wearisome, and confusing . . . it isn't an easy read by any means. Despite that, it *is* probably the most read (and memorized) book in the world.

aÐ℺ aÐ℺ aÐ℺

Let's talk about Mohammed, who was a very interesting man. *Mohammed* means "highly praised" and is the most popular male name in the world even now. The prophet was born in approximately A.D. 570 and became an orphan at a fairly early age. Adopted by his uncle's family, he was basically a happy child despite having lost both his parents and grandfather. At the time he was born, Arabia was in a state of chaos because the various tribes were constantly warring with each other, creating blood feuds and intertribal warfare. The religion at that time was one of animistic polytheism, with many gods and demons, and it hardly exerted any control over morals and social behavior.

As Mohammed progressed through his childhood and teen years, he was looked upon as having a gentle disposition and was always willing to help others. As he grew older, his good deeds earned him titles such as "the True," "the Upright," and "the Trustworthy One." At the age of 25 he wed a woman named Khadija, who was 15 years his senior. The marriage was a good one, and Khadija proved to be one of his most ardent supporters—always there for him through thick and thin.

At one point in a search for solitude, Mohammed turned to a nearby cave to contemplate. While he was there, the voices contacted him for the first time, and he emerged with the phrase that was to reverberate throughout the Arab world: *La ilaha illa 'llah!* ("There is no god but God!"). At first he was certain that he was deranged and even asked his wife whether he was crazy or had actually spoken with God. His wife assured him that he wasn't mentally ill and became his first convert.

Around A.D. 610, Mohammed was convinced that his mission in life was to pass on the message that had been given to him, so he went out to proclaim to the people what God had told him. He was met with derision, insults, persecution, and outrage, and the converts to his message were few. Like Jesus, Mohammed resisted anyone's attempt to make him more than he was . . . which was simply a messenger from God. He claimed only one miracle, that of the

Qur'an itself. (You see, he could barely write his own name, yet over the course of 23 years, he was able to spread the message of a holy book that lasts to this day.)

To say that the reaction to Mohammed's message was hostile is an understatement, for at times it turned to violence and bloodshed. The prophet bucked the existing system by speaking of a monotheistic God—this took away from all the money and sacrifices made to the multiple deities in place at that time, and the hierarchy of priests fought him tooth and nail. In addition, the morals that Mohammed preached were in direct opposition to the licentiousness that was going on with the people, and his teachings on society challenged the unjust order that was in place. He preached that as far as God was concerned, all people were equal.

In the year A.D. 622, the people of Mecca were looking to get rid of this upstart, who they believed had started a revolution. It was at this time that a delegation from the city of Yathrib (later to be called Medina, or "the City of the Prophet") came to Mohammed and said that they'd protect him if he agreed to become their leader. He agreed, and his hazardous journey is known in Arabic as the "Hijra" and is regarded by Muslims as the turning point in world history. (In fact, they date their calendar from the year 622.) The prophet arrived safely and began to administer the city, becoming a renowned statesman and politician. His reputation grew as his tenure became one of justice and mercy.

Over the course of the next several years, there were many battles between Medina and the inhabitants of Mecca. Finally, Mohammed entered Mecca eight years later as a conqueror and immediately dispensed his renowned justice and mercy—and the city of Mecca converted to Islam en masse. He returned to Medina and died in A.D. 632 with almost all of Arabia under his control. He'd succeeded in uniting warring tribes into one people and under one standard. Before the century closed, the prophet's followers then proceeded to conquer Persia, Syria, Palestine, Iraq, Armenia, North Africa, Spain, and portions of France.

Muslims don't want to be called "Mohammedans" because they believe that Mohammed didn't create their religion—God did. So the proper name for the religion of the Muslims is Islam. To call Islam "Mohammedanism" is like calling Christianity "St. Paulism." To the Muslim, God is invisible, but there is no doubt that He exists as the one and only powerful Creator. In the Qur'an they note His awesomeness and earthshaking power. Allah is omnipotent, and it's fair to say that Muslims both love and fear Him.

To help us understand their viewpoint, here's a

passage from the *Spirit of Islam,* which was written in 1891 by Ameer Ali (who claimed to be a descendant of Mohammed):

> [Allah] is the Holy, the Peaceful, the Faithful, the Guardian over His servants, the Shelterer of the orphan, the Guide of the erring, the Deliverer from every affliction, the Friend of the bereaved, the Consoler of the afflicted; in His hand is good, and He is the generous Lord, the Gracious, the Hearer, the Near-at-Hand, the Compassionate, the Merciful, the Very-forgiving, whose love for man is more tender than that of the mother-bird for her young.

Heaven and hell are real to Muslims, but the word *Islam* comes from the root *salam,* meaning "peace," so if the faithful follow the Qur'an, their fear can subside. In fact, the faithful believe that thanks to Allah's mercy, the world of the Qur'an is ultimately a world of joy. There is confidence not only in ultimate justice, but also in help along the way and pardon for the contrite . . . which sounds an awful lot like the God of Judaism.

Like the Old Testament, the Qur'an gives vivid details and not like those stated by the clergy. For example, it's amazing how that book describes much of heaven (which is an actual place to them). Like all the people who have told me about heaven over the past 50 years, the Qur'an describes fountains, gardens, cool meadows where rivers flow, and comfortable cushions to sit upon—in other words, a paradise.

The object of the Qur'an is to present the hereafter in images of such vividness, ". . . that the hearts of those who do not believe in [it] may be inclined to" (6:113). The sharpness of the contrast between heaven and hell is intended to pull the hearer or reader out of spiritual lethargy. The Qur'an puts forth the premise that life is a brief but precious opportunity, offering a once-and-for-all choice; that is, Muslims don't believe in reincarnation, like many Eastern religions do, or in the transmigration of souls (people becoming animals or insects in order to learn).

So, to reiterate, Allah is in many ways like the God of the Old Testament, but to Muslims, He is always just and merciful.

Judaism

Judaic history, although certainly not dull, isn't earthshaking like that of other tribes, such as the indigenous peoples of North America or the clans of the Balkans. The few are always getting conquered by larger groups, and the Jews are no exception.

With conquest comes power and religious influence, and the history of Judaism is filled with invaders and the worship of many different gods from diverse civilizations. In 3000 B.C., for example, the faith was completely overlooked by the large empires of Egypt, Sumeria, and Persia.

Followers were very few in number and roamed the deserts of Arabia as nomads. When they did finally settle in the land of Canaan, it was fairly unimpressive and very small (about one-eighth the size of the state of Illinois), and its terrain was ordinary and somewhat monotonous. So what made Judaism have the influence and impact that it has on the world? In *The World's Religions* (which I highly recommend), Huston Smith writes that "from beginning to end, the Jewish quest for meaning was rooted in their understanding of God."

The Hebrew Bible gives references to other gods, but reading on you see that the Judaic God was the only One—the others are considered to be mortal and not supreme. In the early history of Judaism they called Him El, which later evolved to Yahweh; and he took care of the poor, the sick, and the orphans.

People don't realize that without Judaism and their monotheistic God, we may never have seen Christianity rise up to declare the one God Whom Christ also served. Jews worship one God, and to honor any others is disloyal and tantamount to blasphemy. We see this when Moses came down from the mountain and saw the golden calf—he was so furious he broke the tablets that contained the Ten Commandments, which are also adopted by every Christian church or sect. How, then, could any Christian ever hate a religion that was the forebearer of our beliefs?

And make no mistake about it, the Judaic culture and faith has been one of the most persecuted in the history of humankind. Aside from the Holocaust, Jews were oppressed while under Roman and Egyptian rule, and even today in our supposedly enlightened culture, temples are routinely defaced with swastikas and other insulting graffiti.

In any case, Jews view human beings as helpless (like Job), for their troubles started with their existence and they have no power to stop it. This seems to be fatalism, but deep within they never despair of life, for they believe in their one God Who created them. They also believe that the world is ruled by God, Who has direct intervention in history, and that they are a chosen people who are to live out their plights of good or evil.

Jews also brought prophecy into being. The word *prophet* means "one who speaks with authority of another—one who speaks for God." The writing prophets found themselves in a time that was full of inequities and corruption and had to make their own interpretations, since wealth was concentrated in the hands of the nobility and the rich. As Huston Smith explains, "The prophets come from all classes. Some are sophisticated, others as plain and natural as the hillsides from which they come. Some hear God roaring like a lion; others hear the Divine decree in the ghostly stillness that follows the storm." So the prophets came up with the fact that God can curse or love the people, depending upon how they follow the rules.

Some Jews expect a Messiah that would be God's emissary to help them out of their captivity and persecution. I believe that some followers feel more drawn to the God of Deuteronomy Who has chosen Israel to be separate, and some have extended this into a "Messianic" belief that looks forward to seeing Yahweh or their savior at the end of days. This would be a time when others might get their "just dues" and exalt Israel.

Yahweh is powerful and full of love, but He's intensely interested in all human affairs. To the Jews, God can be a very harsh master, and since they're the chosen ones, God tests them. Judaism is complex because, just like in Christianity, God can be appeased or become cranky or even cruel; He's decidedly good but Divine, powerful and yet humanized—given to jealousy and petulance, but then turns around and gives solace.

Some Jews believe in every word the Torah says and that it was dictated by God, while others don't care or don't believe. The four great sectors of Judaism that show its spiritual side are Faith, Observance, Culture, and Nation. And its followers do approach their religion with more intellectual debate than most other faiths do.

The one thing that keeps God ever present in the Judaic mind and heart is their tradition. All religions have rituals, ceremonies, and the like, but Jews live every day of their lives with it. From getting up in the morning to going to bed at night, ritual plays a very large part in Jewish tradition so as to keep God in everyday life. One of the best ways for Jews to do so is to steep themselves in the history of those who have gone before them.

In her book *A History of God* (another that I highly recommend), Karen Armstrong relates how the Jews turned to their heroes of the past to relate to God:

> One of these distant heroes, venerated in Babylon as an example of patience in suffering, was Job. After the exile, one of the survivors used this old legend to ask fundamental questions about the nature of God and his responsibility for the sufferings of humanity. In the old story, Job

had been tested by God; because he had borne his unmerited sufferings with patience, God had rewarded him by restoring his former prosperity. In the new version of the Job story, the author split the old legend in half and made Job rage against God's behavior.

Christianity

For 2,000 years, Christians have believed that Jesus is God or His son. Note that all other religions look at their messengers as Divine reporters *from* God, but none say that they *are* God. Over the last few hundred years, Christianity has paid little if no attention to God the Father, but focused on Christ—yet in the New Testament, he's called "king of the Jews" or "the son of God," but never once God. And he himself never professes to be God—he always either says nothing at all or acquiesces to the question that he's the Son of God.

Of course other writers in the Bible do state that Jesus is fully God, for example: "[In Christ], the fullness of the Deity dwells in bodily form" (Colossians 2:9). But isn't that true of all of us? That is, if we're all part of God, then God dwells within us all. This isn't to take away the magnificence of Christ's mission, but he can't be—nor is he—our Creator. He comes from our Father and prays to Him . . . not to himself. Also, how could Christ ascend and sit, as they say, on the right hand of God the Father?

Again, we get into the whole theological debate of what to call our Creator and who has the correct truths. It's all so exhausting. As Shakespeare wrote: "What's in a name? That which we call a rose / By any other name would smell as sweet"—but even more important, would smell *the same*. As I've already shared, God has had many names over the history of humankind—not only is it amazing to me that tomes have been written and debated about this, but we don't take into consideration that each language or culture could have their own name springing out of their particular consonants or vowels.

When Jesus prays in Gethsemane, we see an Aramaic endearment being used when he addresses God with his prayer: "Abba, Father! For you everything is possible. Take this cup away from me. But let it be as you, not I, would have it" (Mark 14:36). *Abba* is an Aramaic endearment that would translate in English to something like "Daddy." The most telling is what Jesus tells Mary Magdalene when he appears outside his open tomb (John 20:17): "Do not cling to me, because I have not yet ascended to the Father. But go to the brothers, and tell them: I am ascending to my

Father and your Father, to my God and your God."

Then we have the title of the booklet *The Father Speaks to His Children,* written by Mother Eugenia Elisabetta Ravasio in 1932, which records two apparitions that she received from Father God. One extract from this booklet that I heard when I was in catechism struck me as interesting: "I now repeat My promise which will last forever. All those who call Me by the name of Father, even if only once, will not perish, but will be sure of eternal life among the chosen ones."

Now I'm the first one to accept infused knowledge because I do it in my readings and writings, but I have a problem with this. What if some people have loved God in Turkey, Kenya, or New Guinea and called Him by another name? In the religion of Islam, for instance, to call Allah "Father" is considered blasphemous. Are we led to believe that God cares only for those who call Him "Father"? I think not.

The second part of the message received by Mother Eugenia is much more understandable. It states: "I desire to be known, honored, and loved by all mankind. With regards to honoring me as I desire, all I ask of you is great confidence. Do not think I want great austerities or mortifications [people would whip themselves bloody to be worthy of God]. I don't want you to walk barefoot or to lay your faces in the dust or cover yourself with ashes. No, No! My dearest wish is you behave as My children, simply and trusting in Me."

Even though this is a sweeter message, who's to say that the Jews who kiss the Wailing Wall in Jerusalem, the Muslims who pray toward Mecca by kneeling with their foreheads down on the ground, or the American Indians who use ashes in their sacred rituals are wrong? It seems to rule out how people worship. And of course I know that an all-loving God wouldn't want you to wear hair shirts and defile your body—why would He when He made your body as a temple?

Mother Eugenia's messages are decidedly Catholic, which is all right; after all, who are we to say how someone exercises his or her beliefs is wrong? But then as the message goes on, we see God demanding that we keep Sunday as His day. Since God made all the days, what difference does it make? How about *every* day is a day for God? Church should just be a meeting place to stop off and give love to our Creator and maybe gain some information or help about living life and why we're here. We should then disperse from there and go out and help others . . . not just go out to our cars and forget about God until next Sunday.

Speaking of Catholicism, I'd like to touch on the schisms within it, which began with Martin Luther and King Henry the VIII. Luther was fed up with what he saw as the Church's downsides, including accepting money or property from people trying to buy their way to heaven—and the corruption it brought along with it—so he tacked up his protest on the door of his local parish.

The Protestant movement was largely a protest of the Papal rule or the Greek Orthodox (who are very similar to Catholic but don't accept the Pope). The Reformation brought forth many sects or churches that took up the Protestant cause. I know a lot about the Episcopalians and Lutherans because I was raised in a home that followed the above, as well as Catholicism and Judaism. So as you can see, I started off not just studying, but being part of, these religions. I was presented at temple, then I was baptized in the Episcopal Church and was confirmed by Bishop Spencer in Kansas City. Then later I was baptized Catholic, confirmed by Father Keyes at St. James Church (which still stands—I was even married there), and went on to teach in Catholic schools for 18 years. At one time I was accepted into the Franciscan Order and St. Joseph of Carondelet Order as a nun, but since I wanted to have children, I knew that wouldn't work.

When I took classes for the University of San Francisco at the College of Notre Dame, I still questioned, challenged, fretted, and worried—and the ones who seemed to understand my quest for answers were the Jesuits. I remember doing a reading for the head of the theology department at Santa Clara University. He never said a word while I nervously rattled on about his future, and then right before he left he said, "Sylvia, you are a prophet." I was too nervous at that point to say anything back.

I have to say that the Catholic Church did protect me and let me teach religion with full reign. I even taught the beginnings of magic and brought in the ancient practice of Wicca (among others). When I taught literature, I instructed from the Bhagavad Gita, or about the gods of Olympus and mythology. Sure I threw in *The Catcher in the Rye, Ulysses, The Red Badge of Courage,* and Shakespeare's plays—but then I'd slip in another religious text that didn't have anything to do with Catholicism but had a great deal to do with expanding knowledge.

I saw one of my old students at one of my seminars recently, and I was very happy to hear her say that I'd opened her mind more than anyone. I tried to teach my students the same thing I write and lecture about now: that humankind rushes to forever gratify ourselves with things, leaving our insides weak and unfulfilled. We can see this in religious writings as well as literature.

It seems that many people start out as I did, with one religion or many. From all of the beliefs and moral codes, they either stay under the umbrella that they're first subjected to because it's comfortable or fits their souls, or they begin to rebel and search for a logical basis for all the dogma. (Guess which camp I ended up in?)

I have to say that some of the rules are really ridiculous. Ethics are one thing, but to tell people that if they eat meat on Friday and die on Saturday, they'll go to hell—and then change the rules—is something else. So does that mean that everyone who went to hell (which was supposed to be a place of everlasting fire with no escape) got to come back up when the rule changed that you could eat meat? I feel that if you make a rule, then for God's sake give some thought to it and be consistent. Otherwise we begin to lose faith in the whole system.

Can't We All Just Get Along?

It's sad how so much ignorance prevails in religious teachings—especially when they mix in human-made dogma. For example, true Muslims respect Christ and his saintly mother and even say that he was a great prophet and messenger from God . . . but not so with today's Christians! The sad thing about Christianity now is that it's not Jesus's Christianity, but Paul's. Most religions have a bloody history, but sadly the so-called

Christians are the bloodiest of all. This isn't a criticism, because I'm a Gnostic Christian who follows Jesus's true teachings. (I explain more about Gnosticism in Chapter 4.) We should never attack anyone's beliefs, whether we think ours are superior or not, nor should we be ignorant enough to believe that we could ever completely understand someone else's belief, culture, and creed.

The Islamic faith has a lot of similarities with the Gnostic faith, both in its outlook on God and its respect for and belief in Christ's teachings. On the Website **www.al-islam.com**, I found these words penned by Yasin T. al-Jibouri:

> Everything happens according to a plan put forth by the Planner and Executor of the world, the One and Only God Who created it and everything in it. *Accidentally, coincidentally,* and *by chance* are words and expressions which should be eliminated from language altogether; they are intruders. They are sacrilegious.

These seem to be harsh words, but I can see where he was coming from—after all, it confirms what I've said about our charts of life and what we have chosen for ourselves. There are no "accidents."

It seems that Mr. al-Jibouri lived in the United States for many years and did some investigation of

Christian churches in which he discovered a profound prejudice against Muslims in general when he was subjected to "conversion" tactics. In seeing his faith attacked, he in turn attacked the hypocritical beliefs of the Christians and took as his life's motto Mohammed's traditional saying: "One who remains silent rather than says the truth is a tongue-tied Satan."

I don't know about the Satan part, but I believe that you should show witness to your God by example or by prayer or your form of worship, but do witness your loving Creator. If we all did so and forgot the human-made dogma, we'd be under an ecumenical umbrella. The late Pope John XXIII, bless his heart, was striving for a council where everyone could have that same understanding umbrella to stand under. Could it have been done? Probably not, but God love him for thinking of it and wanting it—although the dream died with him.

Islam is one of the most tolerant of religions, as are the Hindus who live mainly in India. Sure, they've had their uprisings, but Hindus exist side by side with Buddhists, Muslims, Taoists, and Christians. I may not understand the temples dedicated to rats, monkeys, or the elephant god in India, but I do respect their right to their own beliefs. Again, since God made us all, then we give honor and homage to our Creator in our own way and through all aspects.

If we have different cultures and colors that we seem to either ignore or accept, then why do we care how people believe? People should also realize that morality is geographical and cultural. In Kenya, you can have more than one wife; in Uganda, females can walk around bare-breasted; and in the Amazon, males don't cover their penises . . . but try any of that in the "civilized world" and see what happens!

In the Qur'an, it states: "Inform My servants that I am *the* Forgiving, *the* Merciful" (15:49). It's also interesting to note that God's compassion and mercy are cited 192 times in the Qur'an, versus 17 references to His wrath and vengeance. This is a very high ratio in comparison to the Bible, which has many more references to God's wrath. To Muslims, Allah is the only God there is, and who is to deny them that?

Huston Smith put forth more than once that the religion of Islam is probably closer in concept to Western religions (Judaism and Christianity) than any other, yet it's also one of the most misunderstood by the Western world. In fact, all the Eastern religions have nothing but good things to say about Jesus—many called him a prophet and great teacher. Too bad that we don't give them the same courtesy. . . .

Getting back to Christianity, I was once watching a program on CNN when I noticed that some people out there were selling "nails" to hang around one's neck and even "Jesus wrapping paper." *Dear God,* I said to myself, *what are we doing to capitalize on this unfair tragedy to Christ?!* Then a minister came on and said that the crucifix is a sign of death. Now I wear a Templar cross, which you always see me wearing when I make public appearances. Yet I've also worn a pendant with the Arabic sign for Allah and another with the Star of David because they're all positive symbols that have come down to us from people who honored their God.

About 40 years ago, I remember Francine telling my ministers that the one disappointment Jesus had (we're not unhappy on the Other Side, but we certainly have lectures about right and wrong), which he voiced in a lecture, was that he was discouraged that humankind only seemed to remember his bloody body hanging on a cross. He said that hardly anyone remembers or talks about the happy Christ, the teaching Christ, the intellectual Christ . . . only the crucified Christ. I have crosses, but not one has his suffering figure on it.

Francine went on to say that Jesus came to Earth to show honor and love for our omnipotent Father. He wanted to give back the real God in rebuttal to the mean One of the Old Testament. The Jews didn't crucify Christ as such . . . and here we go again with the mentality of "My God is better than your God." Also, do we really want to talk about what persecution the Jews have gone through because they didn't line up with what Hitler believed? Yet it makes me sad to think that Christ's mission was aborted in so many ways. He tried to bring the true God to humankind, and for that he was crucified—which is all we think about or often remember. We forget his parables and beatitudes and concentrate on his death. We forget that he didn't believe in judgment or hypocrites; instead, he lived a good life and honored a loving Father.

❧ ❧ ❧

The big three monotheistic religions have a purpose and a goal. You don't have to be a theologian to hear each one (along with other religions) scream that they're "right" because in God's omniscience, they're *all* right. Does that seem like a contradictory sentence? Possibly, but if you look again at the perfection and all-knowingness of God, He could never do less than accept all his creations *and* the way they believe. I think that the only universal law is to love God and do good, and all the rest will follow. If you want to be a whirling dervish and that's your belief, who are any of us to say that you're wrong? God would never stand at the pearly gates with a notepad and ask you what you practiced (as if He wouldn't know) and only let whom He deemed true to be let in.

Islam, Judaism, and Christianity have another common thread in that they don't believe life is cyclical; that is, they don't accept the premise of reincarnation. Rather, they believe that history had a beginning, and God intervened in it in a certain way to guide it toward an appointed climax. Usually this climax is that the "just" will be let into heaven and the rest will not. Naturally each has its own understanding of what the future will look like and all agree that a Divine future awaits us.

It's interesting to note that many religions don't believe in reincarnation, yet they do believe in an afterlife. If we (as they believe) can become saints or angels, then why couldn't we come back into life and do better the next time? This certainly shows us that God is an "equal opportunity employer," so in His mercy we're not allowed just one life to make or break our progression of our soul. Almost all faiths believe that there is an afterlife, but it's interesting that the three main monotheistic religions of Christianity, Judaism, and Islam won't bridge the gap of having to come back even when simple logic dictates otherwise in explaining the inequities of life.

It's simple then . . . if we live one life or many, why not do so with love and charity, not only for the God outside but for the spark of God within?

Chapter Three

OTHER FAITHS EXPLORED

I'd like to take a moment here to explain that in no way could I (or would I) attempt to present the fullness of any of the world's magnificent faiths. So many offshoots, sects, and denominations have sprung up from these religions that it would fall to experts to collaborate on covering them all . . . and even then I'm sure that others would disagree with their findings. In other words, religion is not only a very complex and all-encompassing subject about which volumes have been written, but it's also one of the most discussed and arbitrary.

Humankind's search for God started with the first step ever taken, and in all likelihood will continue to the end of our days on this planet. With this in mind, I'm going to present a thumbnail sketch of some of the world's major faiths. The interesting things that I've learned in my research are the many similarities that these beliefs have in their philosophies, along with the basic premises that each one has about religious tolerance. The fact that humans haven't always practiced this tolerance is possibly the greatest affront to God ever made—and one in which all of us should work hard to remedy.

Hinduism

Along with being the oldest of the organized religions and greatly God centered, Hinduism is also very much about the human body. In fact, legend says that Buddha found it to be too involved with physicality and not enough about God. I think that's because of the ancient practice of yoga that still goes on today. Some methods, for instance, entail purification fasts, high colonics, and swallowing gauzelike cloth to cleanse the stomach. I admit that these are extreme forms practiced by a select few, but the basic premise of yoga is fueled by the Hindu belief that the body must be sound so that the soul can reside in it in a healthy manner.

Probably the most famous Hindu for most of us was Mahatma Gandhi, a great leader who fought for India's independence from British rule, but a man who also tried to bring about peace between the Hindus and Muslims in India. Through it all, Gandhi advocated nonviolence, which later on inspired others such as Martin Luther King, Jr. Although Gandhi ended up being assassinated, his work and philosophy helped lead to his country's independence and the establishment of two nations: India and Pakistan.

It's hard to summarize Hinduism because of the seeming multiplicity of gods—one can get lost in the sometimes confusing mythology of Krishna, Vishnu, and countless other heroes and deities. As Huston Smith says, "If we take Hinduism as a whole, with its vast literature and its complicated rituals, and try to compress it into a single affirmation, we find the religion saying: you can have what you want."

Hinduism states that people want four things: *pleasure, worldly success, responsible discharge of duty,* and *liberation.* The first two (pleasure and worldly success) are on the path of desire, while the last two (responsible discharge of duty and liberation) are on the path of renunciation. As we'll explore, the Hindu faith shows the tolerance of its philosophy by noting that none of these "wants" are wrong—it's only a question of timing as to which of them an individual pursues.

The religion acknowledges the fact that pleasure is desired by human beings, for we all have sensors for it built into our bodies, yet it asks that we seek it morally and responsibly. Sensual and hedonistic pursuits aren't frowned on; they're actually encouraged within the framework of morality and social laws. The Hindu acknowledgment of the pleasure that human beings need and want is only one part of its overall plan of advancement of the soul, for the faith realizes that there will be a time when the person who only seeks pleasure realizes that that's not all there is.

This is also where the philosophy of reincarnation comes into play, for Hinduism believes that it may take more than one life to advance through the four wants of humankind. Once a soul has discovered that pleasure is not all there is, it advances to the next step, which is usually worldly success, although the two are many times combined because both are on the path of desire.

Hinduism also acknowledges humankind's drives for money, power, possessions, success, and so forth. Wealth and power are competitive; that is, unlike mental and spiritual values, they don't multiply when shared. This makes competition precarious because it can actually destroy success, wealth, and power. Others are also seeking "worldly success," and competition is the by-product that can either lift you up or dash you on the rocks. Now I understand this because money for money's sake is a lonely road, and if you succeed and don't share it, it's either empty unto itself, or you lose it and you're empty anyway.

The drive for success can be addictive, causing spirituality to take a backseat, so it can be a goal without a saturation point. Hinduism realizes that you must earn enough money to support your family and function in the world, but it also knows that there will be a point at which you realize that you can have all the money and fame in the world, yet something's still missing. This is where Hinduism patiently waits to direct you to the next step in perfecting the soul . . . changing you from the path of desire to that of renunciation. It realizes that when you have all that you could ever want, you'll discover that it's still not the be-all and end-all of life. Hinduism knows that you'll then either find fulfillment in serving others (discharge of duty) through philanthropy, politics, or public service; or by seeking God (liberation). To do so, you'll be in a state of renunciation as opposed to desire.

We see people making this renunciation every day, in the successful stockbroker who quits his job and enjoys the simple life of the mountains or seashore, the CEO who lives out her days in a monastery, the renowned doctor who decides to forgo his wealthy practice and go to Africa to work pro bono for a charitable organization, or the famous actress who retires from motion pictures to dedicate her life to taking care of animals or starving children.

The paths of desire (pleasure and worldly success) are based in the self, while those of renunciation (discharge of duty and liberation) are rooted in seeking God. Hinduism knows that everyone will eventually seek the paths of renunciation, even if it takes many lifetimes to do so. The individual soul comes to the realization that wealth and fame don't survive bodily death and that pleasure is fleeting. When it does, it dedicates itself to serving and helping others and seeking God.

The paths of renunciation instruct that all things in this world are transient and that the way to God is through knowledge. The Hindus adore God, but they're concerned that the things of this world deter the path to Him. Patience is the key and the realization that there are many roads to God . . . and many lifetimes in which to find Him.

The myths, symbols, rituals, and hundreds of gods of Hinduism are all very confusing to the outsider and many times misunderstood. Hindus could really be seen as runaways who renounce the successes of life and find their own aloneness with God. I find this quite beautiful, and I think that followers have the right idea that this life's pain and heartache can be withstood because we go back to God. If they don't study deep enough, outsiders might think that Hinduism deals in idolatry and is polytheistic in nature, but that's not true. Instead, their numerous gods are actually only worshiped as aspects of the one Creator, and their statues and temples are merely symbols of these aspects.

The one problem that has always existed in India and Hinduism is the now-outlawed caste system. The regulations of marriage and even social contact have made India by some standards the least tolerant nation in social freedom while still being the most tolerant in views of religious thoughts and ideas.

Another difficulty with Hinduism that the big three monotheistic beliefs of Islam, Judaism, and Christianity have is with reincarnation, since none of them believe in it or advocate it. Hinduism embraces it—in fact, it's one of the most deeply rooted beliefs in the faith, for it's the method in which the soul finds its way to God by gaining knowledge and enlightenment. In the Bhagavad Gita, it says:

> *Worn out garments*
> *Are shed by the body*
> *Worn out bodies*
> *Are shed by the dweller*

The premise of reincarnation also brings karma with it. For the Hindu, karma is very fatalistic, which seems to have no reparation except for living more lives. Nevertheless, Hinduism is truly a religion grounded in God. As Huston Smith writes:

> Is life not more interesting for the varied contributions of Confucianists, Taoists, Buddhists, Muslims, Jews, and Christians? "How artistic," writes a contemporary Hindu, "that there should be room for such variety—how rich the texture is, and how much more interesting than if the Almighty had decreed one antiseptically safe, exclusive, orthodox way. Although he is Unity, God finds, it seems, his recreation in variety!"

It has always been this way with Hindus, for they believe that every major religion is an alternate path to God. It's kind of refreshing to see that a faith can be more concerned with the individual soul than whether it's right or wrong in its dogma. There's a rich texture in all religions, but beyond their differences, the same goal beckons . . . and that really sums up what this book is about. In the search for our Father, we may not like His aloofness, demands, or temperament (which are all human traits), but in the final analysis, who cares? If we come to God trying to do the best we can, what more can we ask than that we're all a tapestry made up of many colors and threads? After all, we each make up the final, finished picture.

Buddhism

Now I'd like to present some information about the beautiful religion and philosophy of Buddhism. To begin to understand this faith, which is somewhat different from most because it doesn't place an emphasis on God, let's first look at the life of its founder, Siddhartha Gautama. Later in life, he was known as Buddha, which means "the one who knows," "the awakened one," or "the enlightened one."

Siddhartha Gautama was born around 563 B.C. in Lumbini, located in northern India near the border of Nepal, to the ruler of a small kingdom of the Sakya clan. His mother died seven days after his birth, so he was raised by his father and his father's second wife. Much of Siddhartha's life has been embellished, and many times it's difficult to separate fact from legend. You see, the story of his origins and teachings were given orally for many years, and writings regarding his existence weren't completed until many years after his death. With that in mind, I'd like to give you a brief history of his life as it's most widely accepted today.

Soon after Siddhartha was born, he was supposedly

examined by holy men who said that he'd either become a great king and political leader or a grand religious leader. As the story goes, his father wanted Siddhartha to follow as his heir and proceeded to provide a life of luxurious upbringing for his son. Fearing that Siddhartha might not become king, his father ordered him to be shielded from all the ugliness of life, such as death, sickness, poverty, and old age.

At around seven years of age, Siddhartha began his instruction in the tenets of Hinduism, as well as the ways of battle. By the time he was 16, he was well versed in the religion *and* quite accomplished in the athletic skills of warfare and weaponry. It was at this time that his father decided it was time for him to marry, so the young prince wed a young woman named Yasodhara, and soon they had a son named Rahula. Siddhartha and his family lived a life of luxury and affluence because his father made it so, but in his early 20s he became discontent, due to his first contacts with the reality of life.

As legend has it, it was at this time that Siddhartha had "four passing sights" with the ugliness of life. The story is told that one day the prince saw a bent and trembling elderly person, and the reality of old age became knowledge. On a second encounter, he noted a sick man suffering from a disease; and on a third, he watched a funeral procession and spied a corpse. Finally, he met an austere monk who had an inner tranquility that suggested to Siddhartha that he'd known happiness along with the ugliness of life.

Siddhartha repeatedly asked questions about the things he saw and got no definitive answers . . . just more pampering by his father. At the age of 29, he was so frustrated that he decided to find things out for himself and renounce his regal life. He left his family and the palace with only a servant, and once he'd gotten far enough away, he exchanged his fine clothes for simple cloth and sent the servant back to his family. Siddhartha was on a quest to find out why people suffer and how to overcome it.

The former prince became a wandering monk and sought knowledge by studying with the well-known Hindu teachers of the day. At last he discovered that he could learn no more from them, so he decided to study under some ascetics, who believed that the body was a hindrance to spiritual development. Siddhartha almost starved himself to death and punished his body in different ways seeking enlightenment, until he ultimately determined that this was also not the way. He began to eat normally again and decided that he'd place himself under a bodhi tree and meditate on the problem until he found the answer. He was determined not to move until what he sought was found—he'd spent six years trying to find enlightenment from others, and now it was just himself.

On a night of the full moon, complete enlightenment came to him, and it was at that moment that he became "Buddha." According to legend, he first had to battle the temptation put forth by "the Evil One" (sounds a lot like Christ being tempted by Satan). Supposedly, the Evil One attacked first in the form of Kama, the God of Desire, parading three beautiful and voluptuous women in front of Siddhartha to rouse him out of his meditation—and he remained unmoved.

Then the Evil One decided to become Mara, the Lord of Death, and had his hosts attack the former prince with hurricanes, torrential rains, and showers of flaming rocks. But so intent was Buddha's focus that all of these attacks turned into flowers when they reached his field of concentration. Desperate, Mara then tried to attack his reason, saying that no one would understand except Siddhartha, so he should just attain Nirvana and leave this earth. Buddha then touched a finger to the earth, which resounded with loud roars of "I bear witness!" causing Mara and his hosts to flee.

The former prince continued to meditate under the tree for another seven days, finally deciding to take his knowledge to those who could understand and to dedicate his life to teaching. He was now 35 years old, and for approximately another 45 years, he dedicated himself to fulfilling his mission until his death at around age 80.

Buddha was known for accepting the downtrodden as part of his following—even against society's unwritten rules, he accepted women and the "untouchables," or the lowest caste of society at that time. He was said to be a combination of wisdom, dignity, friendliness, and kindness; and he never set himself up as an authority figure or a deity. He walked the roads of India seeking out anyone who would listen in towns, cities, villages, or countrysides. He did this nine months out of every year, taking three months (coinciding with the rainy season) to teach in seclusion with his monks. While controversial, Buddha was sought after by both kings and beggars for his knowledge, and the wealthy eventually assisted him in supporting monasteries for his monks in various locales.

The basic precepts of Buddhism are "The Four Noble Truths" and "The Noble Eightfold Path." The first noble truth is basically that suffering colors all finite existence to some degree. The second says that suffering comes from desire for private fulfillment. The third noble truth is that if we lose desire, so will we lose suffering. The fourth shows that the way to ending suffering is by following the eightfold path, or the "Middle Way," which consists of Right Understanding, Right Intent, Right Speech, Right Action, Right

Livelihood, Right Effort, Right Mindfulness, and Right Concentration.

I'm not going to go any deeper into the Buddhist religion other than to say that after the death of Buddha, it split into two groups: (1) the *Theravada,* which is practiced by monks and nuns in monasteries around the world and focuses on the effort to attain Nirvana individually; and (2) the *Mahayana,* which is essentially practiced by laypeople and stresses compassion in helping others. Out of these two basic groups came other offshoots such as Zen Buddhism, but I leave it to you to explore the faith further if you're so inclined.

I myself love Buddhism with its great wisdom, kindness, and philosophy . . . but then I love all religions (or at least parts of them). Critics note that the faith doesn't acknowledge God in any way, and some even say that it's more of a philosophy than a religion. Others claim that because Buddha stated that there is no soul in human beings because all things are transitory, he didn't believe in a higher power. I don't believe this. Whenever Buddha was asked about a higher power, he was either silent or answered by intimating that people needed to know themselves better and deal with life to progress to Nirvana. I believe that Buddha believed in God but didn't bring Him into his teachings because he believed that He was unknowable to human beings and would be a distraction to his teachings of advancing to Nirvana.

I'm going to end this section with this anecdote: When Buddha knew that he was near death, he lay on his right side and asked those around him if they had any questions. All were silent, so he spoke his final words: "All component things decay; work on your own salvation with diligence."

Confucianism

Confucianism has been around for a long time, and was started by a single person who tried to bring prophecy and sensibility to a culture (China) that was floundering and in need of spiritual direction. Confucius was born around 551 **B.C.** in what is now known as the Shandong province of China. Also called "Kung Fu-tzu" or "Kung the Master," there's probably never been any name more associated with China than Confucius. Known to the Chinese as "the First Teacher," which referred to his being the best of all instructors, his teachings have influenced one quarter of the planet's population, up to and including the present day.

His disciples believed that since the beginning of time, there had never been a man such as their master, and many wanted to deify him. Confucius would have none of that; in fact, he actually considered himself a failure for not reaching his goal of changing the social plight of China for good (I'm sure that all true prophets have their own demons of doubt, which makes them more authentic to me than if they believe that they're perfect).

Huston Smith says that Confucius held some government posts (remember that Gandhi was also a lawyer), and his goal was to hold public office—for he believed that his theories wouldn't take hold unless he could *show* that they worked. He gained much acclaim in his posts, which didn't make him very popular with those in charge. And when the ruler of his own state asked him for advice, Confucius replied tartly that he had better learn to govern himself before trying to govern others. Needless to say, the man wasn't too pleased. Because of Confucius's popularity, the ruler didn't have him killed, but he did give the master a hollow title with no power in the hopes of silencing him. Confucius resigned in disgust.

At the age of 50, the master received what he called his "Divine mission." He spent the next 13 years wandering from province to province, trying to advise those in charge on how to help their citizens. He hoped that they'd put his ideas into practice, but that never happened. Even peasants criticized him, so all he had was a small band of followers and disciples.

After a change in administration, Confucius was invited to return to his home. He was too old for administrative office, so he spent the last five years of his life quietly teaching people about China's history. Due to his fairness, lack of corruption, and focus on the people, he was a failure as a politician and became a target of ridicule.

Nevertheless, history has proven Confucius to be one of the world's greatest teachers. In my own humble opinion, his greatness lay in his humanness. For example, he stated that "there are four things in the Way of the profound person, none of which I have been able to do. To serve my father as I would expect my son to serve me [his father died when he was three]. To serve my ruler as I would expect my ministers to serve me [ego clashes from rulers never let this happen]. To serve my elder brother as I would expect my younger brothers to serve me [he had no elder brother]. To be the first to treat friends as I would expect them to treat me. These I have not been able to do."

You see, Confucius was the first to admit his mistakes. He loved to be with people, enjoyed song and drink, and was almost always cheerful—and even though his philosophy might seem commonplace and his place in history an enigma, the clue to Confucius's power and influence lies in viewing his teachings against the backdrop of social anarchy. He tried to bring order and peace to an overbearing regime that he saw was corrupt. Like John the Baptist, he was a voice crying out in the middle of his stiff, strict, and unbending society. (Isn't that what happens when the world seems to go astray? A messenger shows up to try to get human beings back on track.)

Confucius studied history in an attempt to show humankind the follies of past times in order to learn from them, but the powers that be would have none of it. His genius manifested itself in simple ways, such as his proposal for social order, which he said must be a continuum with the past, with the same morals and spirituality that keep people safe in what they know.

The master seemed to warn against rushing into anything, as the wisdom of the ancients was simple and steadfast. He wasn't against progress, but felt that if we advanced too fast, respect and spirituality would be lost. (Doesn't that have a ring of truth now?) He once said, "The true gentleman is friendly but not familiar. The inferior man is familiar but not friendly." And, "The well bred are dignified but not pompous. The ill bred are pompous but not dignified."

The glorification of Confucius came after his death—his wisdom was embraced by almost all of China and was an integral part of their education for more than 2,000 years, until the advent of the

Communist state. Children in every schoolroom would bow to a plaque that commemorated Confucius before they began their studies, and it was this veneration that made historians wonder whether this faith was actually a religion or not. Many considered his teachings to only be those of ethics and social order.

I believe that Confucius was, at the very least, a true humanist. Like most Chinese at that time, he believed that ancestors lived in a heaven that was ruled by Shang Ti, the supreme ancestor; and that when we died, we went from Earth to heaven to live with our ancestors in a more honorable estate. However, this differed with some of the practices that the Chinese did to venerate their ancestors. For example, sacrifice was deemed as necessary to the ancestors and crucial to everyday life, while Confucius felt that we should help those on Earth first and *then* our ancestors. The Chinese also placed great stock in receiving communication from their ancestors in the form of signs, while Confucius thought that wasn't nearly as important as those on Earth who needed help. He didn't try to tear down the belief in heaven; rather, he just changed the focus to those who were currently alive.

The Chinese belief that Heaven is a continuation of Earth isn't that much different from many religions. In fact, there are so many similarities when you break them down and get through the dogma, it all boils down to the same truth: Love God, do good to everyone, and then go Home . . . and, as Confucians say, allow the continuance of life to continue. As one of his famous sayings warned: "He who offends the gods has no one to pray to."

Taoism

Taoism (pronounced "Dow-ism") originated with a Chinese man named Lao-tzu. Said to have been born in the 6th century B.C., Lao-tzu's personality—along with who he really was—is shrouded in mystery. Even his name (which was obviously given as an endearment by his followers) can be variously translated as "the Grand Old Master," "the Old Boy," or "the Old Fellow." There are many legends that surround him, such as the one that claims he was carried in his mother's womb for 81 years and born an old man, or the one that insists that he was born from a shooting star.

Lao-tzu supposedly led a simple, unassertive, and somewhat reclusive life, as opposed to most of the other prophets, who were very much in public life. According to Huston Smith, the first Chinese historian, Ssu-ma Ch'ien, speaks only of the enigmatic impression Lao-tzu left . . . the sense that he possessed depths of understanding that defied ready comprehension.

Over the years, the Old Fellow became saddened when his people didn't embrace or cultivate the natural goodness he advocated. He didn't preach or teach a great deal, and since he sought a greater personal solitude for his closing years, he decided to leave China. As the legend goes, he was stopped at the border by a simple gatekeeper who knew the greatness of the man and his teachings. The gatekeeper tried to convince Lao-tzu to turn back and return to China where he was needed. Lao-tzu would have none of it, as he was discouraged by a civilization that he felt wasn't actually civilized. The gatekeeper then implored him to at least leave some record or writings of his beliefs so that the people could use them.

Lao-tzu listened to this request and then consented to do as the gatekeeper asked. He retired for three days and returned with a slim volume of 5,000 characters entitled Tao Te Ching, or *The Way and Its Power*. This is a book about humans being at home in the universe that can be read in half an hour (or, as some say, a lifetime) and is the basic text of Taoist thought even today.

The enigma of Lao-tzu is that he just rode off into what is now known as Tibet on a water buffalo, leaving only a small volume of his writings behind. He didn't promote it or encourage others to believe it—in fact, he was so unconcerned about how people would take to his text that he couldn't be found to answer questions. Yet emperors managed to claim this elusive figure as their ancestor.

The basic premise of Taoism lies in the three meanings of Tao and the three approaches to power that Taoists follow:

1. First is the *way of ultimate reality*. This Tao we can never truly know because of its ultimate grandeur that can't be explained—it's from which all energy that sustains and life springs from.

2. Second is the *way of the universe,* and it's the power that's in all nature and is the ordering principle behind all life. This Tao "assumes flesh" and is basically the sustaining energy of all living and nonliving things. It's spirit rather than matter, and it flows constantly and can never be exhausted. The more we draw on it, the more it flows.

3. Third is the *way of human life,* when it combines with the Tao of the universe. This way of life is based on the three approaches to power, or *Te.* Taoists have determined that there are three ways that power can be approached, and these three designate the "schools" of Taoism that are practiced today. At first glance they seem very different, but they do bind together in their

primary objective, which is in using Te to obtain their desired goals:

— The first school is philosophical Taoism. This is a reflective and meditative form that believes in using power efficiently in order to conserve it within. A primary principle used here is the concept of *wu wei,* a phrase that translates to "inaction." To the philosophical Taoist, inaction can be quite effective, especially in removing friction from interpersonal relationships, nature, and psychic conflicts.

— There really is no name for the second school per se, but it does deal with vitalizing programs for the body, which has even led to immortality cults within its structure. This second school contains those within it who are involved with training programs to try to increase the amount of power available in utilizing matter, movement, and their minds. Out of this vocation came acupuncture, herbal remedies, tai chi (the program of bodily movement that incorporates dance, meditation, calisthenics, yin/yang philosophy, and martial arts), and Taoist meditation. They also have a form of yoga that was probably brought over to China by Hinduism.

— The third school is religious Taoism, which is the form practiced more than any other. While the philosophical and vitalizing schools have their purpose, they took longer to develop than the religious form did. Humans had to deal with everyday problems, which religious Taoism deals with. It primarily uses power in utilizing rituals and in creating magic—not in the art of illusion, but magic in the true sense of the word . . . meaning to utilize higher powers for use in the visible world.

Suffice it to say that the true Taoist actually practices all forms to one degree or another, so they aren't as far afield from each other as an outsider might think. The Taoist believes that selflessness, cleanliness, and emotional calm are the preliminaries to arriving at self-knowledge, but they must be found in deep meditation. In many ways it seems that it can be somewhat summed up by this stanza from the Tao Te Ching:

Do you have the patience to wait
till your mud settles and the water is clear?

Can you remain unmoving
till the right action arises by itself?

As the Chinese say, Confucius roams within our world and society, while Lao-tzu is the romantic and fantastic, or what transcends the human. The Taoist exists inside, while Confucianism (like Christianity and Islam) exists more on the outside. Taoism resides totally in the self—there seems to be a supreme force, but it's very indefinable and mysterious. Look at it in this way: The less Lao-tzu said, the more people thought and debated about it. At least it got people to even agree to disagree, and none of that is bad.

Although it can be a very beautiful religion, I personally feel that Taoism is too opaque for the general public, but because it has a moral base and a supreme force, God bless it. There's a wonderful passage from the Tao Te Ching that I'd like to end this overview with, for it's a beautiful message about God:

> *There is a being, wonderful, perfect;*
> *it existed before heaven and earth.*
> *How quiet it is!*
> *How spiritual it is!*
> *It stands alone and it does not change.*
> *It moves around and around,*
> *but does not on this account suffer.*
> *All life comes from it.*
> *It wraps everything with*
> *its love as in a garment, and*

yet it claims no honor,
it does not demand to be Lord.
I do not know its name,
and so I call it Tao, the Way,
and I rejoice in its power.

Zoroastrianism

Another religion that bears mentioning is a fairly small one in terms of actual numbers, but it's big on ideas. Zoroastrianism was founded in Persia between 1000 and 1500 B.C., although many put it as far back as 6800 B.C. No one really knows the exact date, but archaeological evidence seems to indicate that it came into being about 3,500 years ago. This religion is one of the world's oldest continuing monotheistic faiths, and followers believe that their doctrines have deeply influenced the Judaic and Christian religions—especially in the areas of heaven and hell, a messiah, resurrection, and final judgment.

The founder of this religion was Zarathushtra (or "Zoroaster" in Greek), and he purportedly received information from God in a highly meditative state that he more or less described as his "mind's eye." The sacred holy book of the Zorastrians is called the "Avesta," along with a collection of hymns called the

"Gathas." The Gathas describe the worship of God, the understanding of right, the cosmic order of things, the promotion of social justice, and the way an individual has the free-will choice between good and evil.

Zoroaster stated that there was a single deity who was supreme: Ahura Mazda. Asha is a form of an all-encompassing law of righteousness, and it's an aspect of Ahura Mazda that was created. In it, humans choose between right and wrong actions to progress to immortality. This is one of the cornerstones of the creed of the threefold path of the Zoroastrian: good thoughts, good words, and good deeds.

Some proponents of the faith also say that there's an evil spirit, Angra Mainyu, who opposes Ahura Mazda. The resulting cosmic conflict involves the whole of creation, including humans, who must choose which to follow—good or evil. It's also believed that evil and Angra Mainyu will be destroyed at the end of time, at which point dualism will also come to an end and goodness will prevail over all. Eventually everything will be purified, and the occupants of hell will be released.

The religion also says that the universe will go through three eras: creation, the present world (where good and evil are mixed, and where people's good works are gradually transforming the world toward its heavenly ideal), and a final state when good and evil will be separated. It also says that a savior will be born of a virgin—but of Zoroaster's lineage—who will raise the dead and assess everyone in a final judgment.

The worship of Zoroastrians includes prayers and symbolic ceremonies that are conducted before a sacred fire, which represents their God. An interesting premise of their faith is that they don't generally accept converts; in other words, one has to be born into it (although this is disputed by some members).

I believe that this religion had a great influence on both the Judaic and Christian religions, as it's certainly older than Christianity and probably just as old as, or even older than, Judaism. And the concepts of heaven and hell and a savior born of a virgin seem very coincidental.

Several things intrigued me when I researched this faith, but the one that I found most interesting is their creed because it so reflects my own Gnostic belief. Zoroaster believed in free-will choice and that the supreme God, Ahura Mazda, was all good. He also spoke of a temporary hell (again something Gnostics can relate to); that good would triumph over evil, but that the evil would be purified (I've always said it would be reabsorbed back into the mass of God); and that reincarnation was a progression to immortality (the Other Side) by making good choices (something I've always subscribed to). I think anyone can see that this particular faith has in all probability influenced many others, at least in some of their basic beliefs.

Baha'i

I've actually attended some meetings devoted to the practice of Baha'i. The Baha'i movement started in 19th-century Persia and has since spread across the globe. It's been rather neglected in Islamic studies because the faith isn't recognized by many Muslims, but Baha'i aims to fill the gap by presenting the history, practices, and origination of different beliefs . . . be they from Eastern religions or Islam.

The Baha'i faith was started by a young merchant by the name of Siyyid 'Ali Mohammed (1819–1850). Originally associated with the Shaykhi sect of Islam, in 1844 'Ali Mohammed proclaimed himself to be the Báb ("gate" or "door") to the hidden Imam, or leader. In 1848, one of the Báb's disciples, Mirza Husayn Ali, assumed the title of "Bahá'u'lláh" (Arabic for "glory" or "splendor") at a gathering of the Báb's followers. The Báb later confirmed this title, which would be significant later on.

The first followers were mainly drawn from the Shaykhi school and were called "Bábis." This movement advocated an emphasis on inner truth and claimed that the hidden Imam existed not on Earth, but in a spiritual phenomenon of the unseen world until he was needed. As you can see here, so many (if not all) religions are offshoots of other faiths (in this case, Islam) or ideas.

This shows the many aspects of God—just as there are many facets to us. Unfortunately, many of them go astray thanks to humans' greed or misinterpretation.

The Báb put forth his teachings of the coming of a second messenger in his work *The Bayan,* which is the faith's primary text. This second messenger was the 12th and final Imam, who'd been waiting to bring the world the final truth when it was needed most.

Siyyid 'Ali Mohammed was arrested and tried as a rebel, and he was sentenced to death by firing squad, which was carried out in 1850. A very interesting side note to this execution was that earlier in the day, the Báb had warned the guards that no "earthly power" could silence him until he'd finished all that he had to say. The firing squad was made up of 750 riflemen in tiered steps of 250 each, and when they initially fired to kill the Báb, gun smoke filled up the yard of the barracks where the execution was taking place. The firing squad and some 10,000 onlookers who had perched themselves on the walls to witness the execution were blinded. After the smoke cleared, there was no sign of the Báb. Onlookers said that he'd ascended, but guards found him shortly thereafter, giving final instructions to one of his followers in a nearby building. As the guards were again taking him into custody, the Báb calmly announced: "Now you may proceed to fulfill your intention."

In the interim period, Husayn Ali was also imprisoned and then exiled because he followed the Báb. It was during this time that he got his first revelations from God. He finally gave up involvement in the fortunes of the Bábi movement and decided to go his own way. He confided to the other Bábis that he'd had revelations and was on a Divine mission.

Husayn Ali wrote *The Hidden Words, The Seven Valleys,* and *The Book of Certitude,* which became part of the Baha'i scripture. He continued to write and receive revelation as the promised one foretold by the Báb, named "Bahá'u'lláh." The new faith was called Baha'i because of these revelations, and his writings became the cornerstone—thus, another prophet was born. In all, the writings of Bahá'u'lláh comprise more than 100 volumes, which include texts on mystical, social, and ethical teachings.

In a mystical experience, the Bahá'u'lláh wrote (note the pronoun *she*):

> While engulfed in tribulation I heard a wondrous, a most sweet voice, calling above my head. Turning my face, I beheld a maiden, the embodiment of the name of my Lord suspended in the air before me . . . pointing with her finger unto my head, she addressed all who are on earth, saying: By God! This is the best-beloved of the

worlds and yet ye comprehend not. This is the beauty of God amongst you, and the power of His sovereignty within you, could ye but understand. This is the mystery of God and His Treasure, the cause of God and His Glory unto all who are in the kingdom of revelation and of creation, if ye be of them that perceives. This is He whose Presence is the ardent desire of the denizens of the Realm of Eternity and of them that dwell with the Tabernacle of glory and yet from His Beauty do ye turn aside.

Bahá'u'lláh was in exile and a prisoner for much of his life in Palestine. The famed Orientalist Edward Granville Browne visited him there in 1890, and Bahá'u'lláh told him: "Thou hast come to see a prisoner and an exile. . . . We desire but the good of the world and the happiness of nations; yet they deem us a stirrer-up of strife and sedition worthy of bondage and banishment . . . that all nations should become one in faith and all men as brothers; that the bonds of affection and unity between the sons of men should be strengthened; that diversity of religion should cease, and differences of race be annulled—what harm is there in this? . . . Yet so it shall be; these fruitless strifes, these ruinous wars shall pass away, and the 'Most Great Peace' shall come . . . "

Simplified, the Baha'i belief is in one God, but He is always hidden from us and we will never set eyes upon Him. God created the world to make Himself known by us, and all of creation reflects God. The cornerstone of their teachings is acceptance of Bahá'u'lláh as the true manifestation of God that will bring about world peace and humanity. Yes, the practice has rules of right living and a hierarchy of council that deals with all matters of faith, but it certainly isn't what I call an interfering religion. It's rather low-key, as people meet in homes and go over the teachings of the Báb and the Bahá'u'lláh.

The Baha'i have a very easy religion because their rules aren't so strict, and followers genuinely seem to want to love and serve God. There just seems to be so much shrouded in mystery in it, such as their belief that we can't know what the other world (the Other Side) is like. It's not a criticism, but the faith just seems unfinished to me. I found myself with more questions than answers, but then again I didn't study it for years either.

At one meeting I asked, "Why couldn't we know God?" And I was told that it was beyond my (or anyone's) comprehension. I wanted to say more, but kept quiet because no one wants to hear someone else's opinion about their own beliefs. It's easy to fall into the trap of getting on our high horse and either trying to convert others, or at the very least giving reasons (that in our own mind put theirs to shame) why we believe as we do. So I told myself, *Remember that you're here to learn*. I felt the same way in catechism and theology classes in college and in my Christian marriage class. I was one hell of a nuisance.

I have some dear friends who are Baha'i who have never had any problem with me at their meetings, and I certainly admire them. I also appreciate the Bahá'u'lláh's central message for humankind. He wrote: "The best beloved of all things in my sight is justice," and "The earth is but one country, and mankind its citizens." He also put forth the following as a cure for an ailing world: "The well-being of mankind, its peace and security, are unattainable unless and until its unity is firmly established."

Tying It All Together

We can wade through all the world's faiths, only to find that people in the same religion disagree (that's why we see so many spinoffs) and that the truth about God will continue to be debated as long as humans exist on this planet. From the time we could put pen to paper or chisel to stone, we've had every opinion about

God . . . some worth researching and others so opaque that we'd fall into a sea of words.

It's almost as if so many theologians feel that the more they drone on, the more intelligent they'll seem. I feel that true intellect is (or should be) understandable to the masses—after all, Christ, Mohammed, Buddha, and Confucius all talked to people on equal ground, whether it was through examples and stories or just making them feel that their own loving God was close and caring.

Notice that there is a common denominator that runs quite prominently through all these messengers. There's no malice, but there *is* a definite emphasis placed on righteousness in action and thought, and they didn't take inhumanity lightly. Confucius wasn't so esoterically spiritual as Christ, Buddha, or Mohammed, but they all had the universal commandments from God honed to a fine art. They were all very humble and sometimes self-deprecating as well, showing that they had no ego unto themselves. They had a true "I Am," but not a false sense of themselves that they were bigger than life and had all the right answers. But these messengers *did* have the right answers, simple as they were, which were profound and have lasted the tests of centuries.

Regardless of these overviews of the world's religions, which like I said are so minute when compared to the tomes that have already been written about them, discover the parts that fit with you and leave the rest. All of the messengers used those who went before them and either tried to improve on their teachings or gave them their own spin of enlightenment. Who's to say that the way we love and honor God is wrong, as long as we do love and honor Him? After all, the Father of Jesus is also the same God of Mohammed— and He is the Creator of Confucius, Hindus, Jews, Christians, Buddhists, Muslims, Polynesians, Africans, Asians . . . in other words, everyone.

Christians, Muslims, and Jews can affirm many important truths about this great God together, including His oneness, eternalness, power, and majesty. As the Qur'an puts it: "[He is] the Everlasting . . . the All High, the All-Glorious" (2:255). We should never condemn anyone else's way of worship.

To understand how God works, I'd like to share this story from Richard Selzer's *Mortal Lessons:*

> I stand by the bed where a young woman lies, her face postoperative, her mouth twisted in palsy, clownish. A tiny twig of the facial nerve, the one to the muscles of the mouth, has been severed. She will be thus from now on. The surgeon had followed with religious fervor the curve of her flesh; I promise you that. Nevertheless, to

remove the tumor in her cheek, I had to cut that little nerve.

Her young husband is in the room. He stands on the opposite side of the bed, and together they seem to dwell in the evening lamplight, isolated from me, private. Who are they, I ask myself, he and this wry-mouth that I have made who gaze at and touch each other so generously, greedily? The young woman speaks.

"Will my mouth always be like this?" she asks.

"Yes," I say, "It will. It is because the nerve was cut."

She nods, and is silent. But the young man smiles.

"I like it," he says. "It is kind of cute."

All at once, I *know* who he is. I understand, and I lower my gaze. One is not bold in an encounter with a god. Unmindful, he bends to kiss her crooked mouth, and I am so close I can see how he twists his own lips to accommodate to hers, to show her that their kiss still works.

Isn't that what it's really all about—the glimpse of God that we see in everyone everywhere? Whether we're Jewish, Muslim, Protestant, Hindu, Catholic, Buddhist, in a Kenyan tribe, or a member of any other ethnic or religious group, we should try to accommodate, love, trust, and be generous, no matter how the road twists or turns. And then we'll all end up, as my grandson says, "In God's house."

~~ ~~ ~~ ~~ ~~

Chapter Four

THE GNOSTIC PHILOSOPHY AND NOVUS SPIRITUS

As I've taken you through the world's various religions, it may have seemed that I'm biased against Christianity, but that isn't true. I actually feel that I'm a true Christian, but like all Gnostics, I embrace *all* religions and creeds—we're just against anyone putting their own spin on what Jesus Christ had to say.

The history of the Gnostic movement is very old, and the faith had to be hidden many times because of persecution. Elaine Pagels has written several books that contain a great deal about Gnosticism, and her approach is like the scriptures themselves—that is, she addressed her books from a purely academic standpoint, with no prejudice or emotion attached, which makes it more palatable.

All religions are built on other thought and philosophies, and Gnosticism is no different. Yet the faith is also built upon seeking because it's born out of the Essene sect, which Jesus belonged to after years of studying many other religions in his "lost" adult years. (For more on this part of Jesus's life, please see my book *Secrets & Mysteries of the World*.)

In this chapter, I'd like to illuminate my faith for the rest of you.

The Gnostic Story

Long before Christ was an Essene, the beginnings of Gnosticism existed. My spirit guide Francine says that pockets of believers rose up in early Egyptian times around the time of the pharaoh Akhenaten (who put forth the concept of one God in Egyptian history). The word *Gnostic* means "knowledge" or "seeker of truth" and was not an organized movement in its early days. Believers existed in small groups or sects that studied and accumulated written texts and oral traditions for many centuries, and they began to be known during the 3rd century.

In the beginning, most Gnostics were just individuals seeking knowledge who drifted together in groups out of their passion for truth. As time went on, however, these small gatherings started to become communities, such as the Essenes or early Gnostic Christians. Being a Judaic sect, the Essenes lived in fear of being discovered by the Judaic ruling body because their teachings were more in line with Christ's (who later melded into their community because of their beliefs). The early Gnostic Christians evolved out of the beginnings of Christianity and the chaos of the early Christian church, which then evolved into Catholicism.

Being somewhat rebellious in their thinking and philosophy, both Gnostic groups started writing down their teachings to make sure that they were preserved for future generations. Being free thinkers, they also knew that the ruling hierarchy of whatever religion they belonged to wouldn't necessarily be happy with their writings, so they started putting them into containers and burying them.

Some of these documents were found near the Dead Sea, so they were labeled "the Dead Sea Scrolls," while still others were unearthed at Nag Hammadi in Egypt. While both of these were made public, others were kept in hiding to preserve them from the zealous purging of the Catholic Church.

As the Website **www.1gnostic.com** states: "[The Gnostic Gospels], discovered in 1946 at Nag Hammadi in Egypt, disclose a kind of Christianity that is different from the Catholic/Protestant religion based upon the 'orthodox' New Testament, and reveal an approach that may, in fact, be as old if not older than what is now called Christianity."

This site echoes what Francine said many years ago (records of which are in our research library), almost fitting her words to a T, and explaining our faith better than anything I've ever read: "This Gnostic Christianity invites all people to seek within themselves a deeper sense of self that leads ultimately to the revelation that within each of us is a 'True Self' that is a spark of divinity."

What Gnostics Believe

We Gnostics also believe in reincarnation and that we have many lifetimes to formulate our perfection. This keeps our souls on track and helps us ascend in knowledge by seeking more information. In addition, we feel that the body has a cell memory that carries over many phobias and unresolved issues from the past that can be released. Hypnotic regression can help, but asking God to surround us with the white light of the Holy Spirit every morning and night is also very effective to aid us in shrugging off these heavy overcoats of pain and fear carried over from other lifetimes.

We believe in a spirit guide that follows us through life and nudges us along our path. We know that we're attended to by angels that are sent from God to protect us. We feel that Earth is hell—it's a negative place to learn, and when our lives are completed for our soul's perfection, we go Home and stay there. Home is the Other Side, which resides approximately three feet higher than the topography of Earth yet features the same beautiful edifices that this world does. (It also has different places where we research, learn, play, talk, teach, lecture, have concerts, and are in eternal bliss with God.)

We're aware that evil exists and that there are some souls who chose to separate from God at creation—these are the dark entities of this world. But we're also certain that these dark entities are in the Divine plan of God and are needed so that we can see by their negative example how much better we can and will be by doing good.

We don't believe in eternal damnation, even for dark entities, for we know that at the end of the reincarnation schematic, they'll be absorbed back into God's merciful goodness. We, on the other hand, will keep our individual identity because we've developed our "True Self," the one that we charted to gain our perfection and learn for ourselves and God.

In the Gnostic approach, God is known within the "True Self." The world isn't viewed as a positive place (as I stated, it's hell), but it's been driven into sin by the acts of human beings. Gnostics don't necessarily think that all human beings are sinners, but rather that the world itself is just a learning place for the "True Self." The Earth plane is deficient in the love and moral sense that's at the heart of a loving God. As **www.1gnostic. com** states:

> . . . only when one touches their innermost "True Self" does serenity and love truly become known to each person. For Gnostic Christians, Jesus Christ is a revealer of this "True Self" that is Divine, and leads people into an awakening of their true nature. [This is an infusion of the truth of life and God-centerness and why we're here.]
>
> In the Gnostic Gospel of Thomas, Jesus says: ". . . if you do not become acquainted with yourselves, then you are in poverty, and it is you who are the poverty." The core issue is . . . what do you know about you? After all, if you don't know yourself who you walk with every day, how can

you presume to know God who you have never seen or touched, and exists in ways that only your "True Self" can tell you? That is the essence of true spirituality—not just a religion!

The "True Self" here means the simple infusion of the soul that we were born with . . . but then we're thrown into rules and dogma and make God mean and humanized. We come in directly from the Other Side with innocence again and again, and each time we're tested with countless barrages of brainwashings.

From the beginning, Gnostic Christianity has tried valiantly to expose this truth and failed because the ruling political norms of religion smacked it down, saying that this faith didn't have enough rules to keep people in line. Then, of course, there's always the issues of money and pomp and ceremony.

So even though we Gnostics are called a religion for the sake of the law, we're actually a society of people who have come together to establish a love of our Mother and Father God. This is what the Knights Templar tried to protect (among other things), as did parts of the Masons and the Rosicrucians. These sects have so much Gnosticism ingrained in them— and it isn't that they're necessarily secret, but for years it was better to keep their beliefs silent than to be persecuted.

Again, **www.1gnostic.com** states:

> Gnostic Christianity is not just the same old Christian concepts repackaged. It is an approach to spirituality that is radically different from the common Christianity that is in churches all around the [world]. Gnostic Christianity expands the Bible to include other Gospels such as The Gospel of Thomas, The Gospel of Truth, and The Gospel of Philip—each as old as the New Testament witness, but from a different perspective. The emphasis is not on doctrine or dogma, but rather on self-exploration and awakening oneself to a deeper spiritual reality.
>
> If you have ever thought that perhaps religion has been more about control and power than about truth, then perhaps you are a "closet Gnostic." Gnostic Christianity was uprooted in the early centuries because it spoke against oppressive ecclesiastical forms and the dominant "atonement theology" [that you need to do penance for all your sins] that is practiced in "orthodox" Christianity. Today, just as almost two thousand years ago, Gnostic Christianity stands outside of Catholicism and all the various forms of Protestantism—evangelical, mainline, liberal, and fundamentalism—as a resurrected voice

that speaks of a different way, with beautiful and sacred writings that tell of a Christianity that may have been much closer to the heart of Jesus than anything that has been seen in many centuries.

Along with Jesus, Gnostic Christians accept and admire Buddha; Mohammed; Confucius; Lao-tzu; the Báb and Bahá'u'lláh; Mahatma Gandhi; Martin Luther King, Jr.; Mother Teresa; St. Francis of Assisi; Edgar Cayce; Joseph Smith; Vishnu; Pope John XXIII; and on and on it goes, with each one building upon the next.

We believe in a *perfect,* omnipotent God, and we'd never try to convert you—but we do ask that you explore for your own soul's peace. Once you grasp what your personal beliefs are, then you'll get the simple truths . . . and all the guilt will drop from you like a heavy load of bricks.

Guardians of the Truth

Another thing that sets Gnostics apart is the way they've guarded some of history's greatest secrets. For example, they protected the truth about Jesus's death, marriage, and children; along with the worship of Mother God and our all-loving Father. Sacred texts were hidden in monasteries of the Gnostic sects or placed in the care of secret Gnostic societies, which were called by other names to stay out of the limelight.

You see, in the early years of Christianity (and during the Inquisition), people who were branded heretics were killed and martyred. Yet now, thanks to the books *Holy Blood, Holy Grail; The Messianic Legacy;* and *The Da Vinci Code,* the world is ready. In the latter work, author Dan Brown speaks of the Society of Scion, the Illuminati, the Society of the Rosy Cross, and other Gnostic societies that are in places all over the world, but many are still hidden for fear of reprisals. How you could be punished for worshiping a loving God is beyond my comprehension, except that it flies in the face of the establishment of fear . . . and through fear, you gain the power to rule the masses.

It's interesting that many historians now argue that Mary Magdalene was one of Christ's disciples and not a prostitute at all (something that Francine told me almost 50 years ago). They also agree with what I wrote about in *Mother God*—that she was the first of a long line of female priests who aided in the start of the early Gnostic Christian church.

The proof for this groundbreaking theory is painted into Leonardo da Vinci's *The Last Supper* (also pointed out by Dan Brown in his book). If you look closely at the picture, it leaves no doubt that the person to the right of Jesus is a woman.

Thomas Darby, Ph.D., a professor of religious history based in London, has spent the last 15 years researching these claims. He cites numerous historical texts (not just Gnostic writings) that provide clues to the fact that there was once a totally female priesthood for which Mary Magdalene was the first member. This aspect of early Christian history that was brutally suppressed and struck from official records in the 1500s is another reason why the Gnostics went into hiding. It's interesting to note that shortly after this came the witch hunt by the Church that almost decimated the female population . . . which I'm sure was no accident.

As Darby explains: "During the furor surrounding the Protestant Reformation, the Church felt a desperate need to define itself . . . self-definition involved eradicating all traces of anything that didn't fit into church orthodoxy—including the existence of a female priesthood, a secret that has been kept alive by the Gnostic groups since the first century."

In the early days of the Church, these groups created secret societies around the fringes of the central clergy's authority. Because they defied the Church's rule, the Gnostics were rooted out from their hiding places, and they were often persecuted as heretics and burned at the stake.

Francine stated many years ago that most of the first martyrs killed by the Romans were not just

Christians, but Gnostics who dared to go against the Church's hierarchy, which coincided with Roman rule to get rid of these heretics.

Yet with the feeling that hope springs eternal, the Gnostics who made it through were diligent about protecting the writings that did survive. If they couldn't write, then they passed down the traditions orally to the ones who could—or who were artistic enough to encrypt the truth so that someday, someone would understand it all when the world became tired of all the rules and began to look for some honesty in all the morass of dogma.

One such Gnostic student was Leonardo da Vinci, who, according to letters and manuscripts unearthed by Darby, encoded his beliefs in many of his paintings. But the professor goes on to relate that the greatest evidence of all is Mary Magdalene seated beside Jesus at the Last Supper: "[A] close inspection of each of the apostles reveals that the sixth figure from the left is a female. According to da Vinci's own letters, he wanted her to represent Mary Magdalene. The painting itself is proof not only of da Vinci's Gnostic leanings, but demonstrates clearly that Christ himself may have ordained women as his priests."

The Gnostics also knew that Jesus married Mary Magdalene and had children with her, and that the family eventually went to France after the Crucifixion.

Yet the apostles were jealous of her and remarked many times about Christ kissing Mary Magdalene. It's really disconcerting to see that nothing changes in human behavior with jealousy rising even in the midst of a great mission.

Jesus was the first Gnostic who was scourged and martyred . . . whether you believe that he died on the cross (I don't) is your prerogative. Christ's "death" was of high importance to Gnostics, but for reasons that most don't know or believe in. The fact that our Lord was so humiliated and put in so much pain causes outrage among Gnostics, but not guilt over his dying for our sins—because they know that he survived the Crucifixion.

This information is so controversial and dangerous because it could destroy Christianity as we know it today (but not Gnostic Christianity). This monumental truth is being fed to the general public in little doses right now, and I'm sure that all the non-Gnostic churches are raising their defenses and getting ready to attack these facts with all they've got in the interest of survival.

It's so sad that the history of Christianity is covered in blood. I feel that the lowest of the low was the killing of so many women for being witches and even more people in the "burning times" of the Inquisition. Some say more were murdered then than were killed in the

Holocaust, and certainly more than the "terrorists" of today have killed in the name of Islam. And these numbers don't even take into consideration the various "crusades" of early Christianity in which so-called holy minions did nothing but rape, pillage, and murder, all with the alleged aim of regaining the Holy Land.

Be reasonable now, you devout Christians, and don't get your dander up. There's a lot of evidence that has been, and is still being, uncovered regarding Jesus's survival of his crucifixion. (I touched on some of it in my book *Secrets & Mysteries of the World,* so I won't be redundant and espouse it here.) As I said earlier, if you want to believe that Jesus Christ died on the cross for our sins, that's your prerogative, and who am I to tell you how to believe? I only bring this matter up because it's a truth that's been hidden for hundreds of years by Gnostics, but it's slowly coming out to the general public.

Look at how the Catholic Church recently changed its stance on Mary Magdalene's being a prostitute—this is only the tip of the iceberg, and more evidence will be released over time. Books like the aforementioned *Holy Blood, Holy Grail; The Da Vinci Code;* and *The Messianic Legacy* would not and could not have been published years ago, as they would have been considered heresy and the authors persecuted. It was only 60 or so years ago that books were burned by

Hitler's fanatical followers, and even today legions of volumes are on the "banned" lists of many churches.

The Birth of Novus Spiritus

When you're looking for a religion or belief to follow, be sure that you find what simplistically fits you. If you like strict dogma and rules and regulations to adhere to, then go for it. If you want to love God freely and spiritually with no religion attached, then go for that. In other words, there are no wrong choices here, for if you truly want to worship God, He doesn't care what doorway you enter through as long as your motive is pure. Yet He will love you regardless, just as He loves everyone in creation, no matter what faith someone subscribes to (or doesn't).

As you know, it wouldn't be like me to write about so many other religions without telling you about my own. Before I start, however, I can't repeat this too many times: *Take with you what you want and leave the rest.* There are several reasons why I say this, especially since our church's purpose is to give as much as we can to help others through our teachings. We're sure enough in our beliefs to let them stand on their own, so we don't try to convert anybody.

However, we *do* try to help people, for we'd rather have them take some truth than none at all. So if they don't agree with us on all of our teachings, but like some of it and embrace it, then we feel that we've helped them, and we're happy. We teach religious tolerance, feeling that all faiths have some truth—and we've even incorporated those truths ourselves whenever we've found them to augment or confirm what we've already found.

My group is a Gnostic Christian one, but in order to have it sanctioned by the federal and state governments as a religion and a nonprofit organization, I had to come up with a name to operate . . . thus, *Novus Spiritus,* or "New Spirit."

Sometimes we become so overly civilized that we fail to really see the clouds, sunsets, or seasons, and we forget to smell the coffee or the roses. So, after many years of listening to the philosophy of my grandmother and hearing about so many people's search for truth, I began to research the Essenes and their Gnostic philosophy.

Fifteen years before Novus Spiritus began, we were a nonprofit research organization involved in paranormal activity, and that work is still going strong today. During those initial years, I began to establish reciprocity with doctors, scientists, police departments, charities, and the like. I've always felt that a holistic or research center should be a handmaiden to society—and strangely enough, the world of religion has never ostracized me, nor has the world of science ever turned against me.

I stepped out on the stage of the Flint Center near San Jose, California, 18 years ago and said, "I'm going to start a religion or a society that will be by the people, for the people."

The audience was silent and then began to clap, but I could almost read their minds asking, *What in the world is she doing now?* My family was also somewhat taken aback—not because they didn't know where my heart was and that for 50 years I'd been gearing up for this, but it was almost as if they hoped I'd just forget about it. Wasn't it enough that I had a whole organization to run, along with research and readings and helping to solve criminal cases? And now I wanted to open myself up to more criticism? A woman—a psychic at that—starting a religion . . . especially one that had love as its base had to be doomed to fail.

That last part didn't come from my family, but from my colleagues, who told me, "You have to have a fear trap because love doesn't sell."

"What the hell do you mean by 'sell'?" I'd say, beside myself. "How about just telling the truth, which Christ tried to put forth?"

Then the words of John Paul, my dear mystical

friend who's since passed away, came to the foreground: "Be careful, Sylvia, for with your philosophy there are many ways to be crucified." *So be it,* I silently replied, *but if I don't fulfill this mission I might as well die, because it is the essence of me.*

We began by giving intensive research and philosophy classes almost every night to about 70 ministerial candidates. This included everything from creation to reincarnation, spirit guides, the Gnostics and how they got started, and intensive hypnotherapy classes. This went along with all types of paranormal phenomena about death and dying, marriage and grief counseling, the sacraments and what they meant, and myriad other subjects necessary for counseling and helping our fellow human beings. We were declared a formal religious organization by the government, and we were on our way.

It was slow going at first, and many individuals would attend services to see if I'd "be psychic." When they found out that wasn't going to happen, some dropped off, but then people began to see it and get it.

Then we started study groups after I wrote my *Journey of the Soul* series of books, and now they number in the thousands. I have to give huge kudos to Hay House, who had enough guts to publish *Adventures of a Psychic,* which ended up staying on the bestseller list for 59 weeks. (God bless them always for that.) Now we hold worship services in rented halls or community centers. Services are simple, with a prayer and informative sermon, then petitions are heard and put out to Mother God, followed by a closing prayer and social interaction afterward. In addition to doing services, our ministers go to our offices and answer spiritual questions, work the prayer lines, correspond via e-mail, do healings, and visit local nursing homes.

For 14 years I supported it all . . . Novus Spiritus, which was previously known as the Nirvana Foundation, and the Sylvia Browne Corporation. The corporation takes care of all the mundane business stuff such as appointments for my son Chris and myself to do readings, hypnosis appointments for my staff of hypnotists, travel arrangements, seminars, accounting, printing, mailouts, e-mail, and other business-related tasks and expenses.

Novus Spiritus takes care of the spiritual and religious side with their crisis lines, prayer line, spiritual counseling, religious services, study-group support and monitoring, spiritual correspondence, sacraments, ministering to the elderly at various homes and institutions, death and dying counseling, visiting the sick, and so forth. (As an aside, instead of building a church, why don't all faiths build facilities for the elderly, children's centers, or low-cost or free clinics for medical care? Wouldn't that give more glory to

God than spending one hour once a week in a place that isn't used every day? How much more glory can we give to our Father than to help those who need us?)

I personally still work hard doing readings, giving salons to groups of 30 to 50 people on spiritual subjects and philosophy, and giving lectures on various topics all over the United States. I now travel the world as well, including Turkey, Greece, Egypt, Australia, and Canada; and I have plans to go to Tokyo, South Africa, and the United Kingdom.

People say, "You're 70 years old—aren't you going to retire and slow down?" Hell, no! I have my health, except for a split in my right hipbone that acts up. It's not the ball joint, but a crack in the bone thanks to my first husband, but I look at it as a reminder not to make that same mistake again. Francine tells me that there's a type of plasmic glue substance that will come out to fix it. There are times it doesn't hurt as much, but I sometimes see myself walking kind of ducklike— so attractive!

I come from a long line of ancestors on both sides who lived into their 90s (oh God!), so I figure that I have about 20 more years. When people ask why I write so much and so fast, I answer that I have to get it all out before I return Home. Yes, Chris will take up the gauntlet after I go, and perhaps he'll continue with more research (or my ministers will), so Novus Spritus will still grow. Gnosticism has always been a living, active, breathing, searching society—a body of beliefs that keeps being added to by the questions that need answering . . . and when will it ever be the case that there aren't any more questions?

If individuals who believe in our philosophy ask me what they should do about their friends or family members who don't believe, I say, "Leave them alone and let them believe the way they want, because Novus Spiritus is a belief by example rather than dogma." Once the loved ones realize that there's nothing threatening going on, they usually become more accepting and might listen to some of the philosophy or even embrace it themselves.

I don't blame friends and family members for their worry or skepticism, especially with all of the groups that have been profiled in the media as "stealing" or "brainwashing" loved ones. If someone you care about joins a group such as the "Moonies" or certain sects of the Hare Krishnas, how do you know if you'll ever see him or her again? Well, with some groups, you don't . . . but you never have to worry about Novus Spiritus or me.

ঽ৵ঌ ঽ৵ঌ ঽ৵ঌ

I know that it can be difficult for many of you to accept some of the truths I've presented in this chapter—after all, you're fighting 2,000 years of religious instruction, albeit by an institution that has a bloody and corrupt history. Christian churches have a lot of money and power, which can certainly put pressure on you to think the way they want you to. It's difficult to buck the system, for doing so can elicit derision, ridicule, taunts, prejudice, bias, dislike, fear, and hate. Yet all of this is bearable to me, for I love Father and Mother God and Jesus Christ, and I know in my heart and soul that they love me.

Does God care about the truth? Of course He does, for truth brings us closer to Him and what He is all about. God will never stop loving you, will never condemn you, and will always welcome you Home. To stay on track, as I've said so many times, just love God, do good for your fellow human beings, and then shut up and go Home. And don't go humbly to Him—stand tall and proud because you're from divinity.

I'd now like to list the Tenets of Novus Spiritus that were derived from our Gnosticism, with the help of Francine, for I believe that great wisdom lies within them. (For a closer examination of these 21 edicts, please refer to my book *If You Could See What I See*.)

1. The way of all peace is to scale the mountain of self. Loving others makes the climb down easier. We see all things darkly until love lights the lamp of our soul.

2. Whatever thou lovest, lovest thou.

3. Do not give unto God any human pettiness such as vengeance, wrath, or hate. Negativity is man's alone.

4. Create your own heaven, not a hell. You are a creator made from God.

5. Turn thy power outward, not inward, for therein shines the light and the way.

6. In faith be like the wind chimes: Hold steady until faith, like the wind, moves you to joy.

7. Know that each life is a path winding toward perfection. It is the step after step that is hard, not the whole of the journey.

8. Be simple. Allow no man to judge you, not even yourself, for you cannot judge God.

9. You are a light in a lonely, dark desert who enlightens many.

10. Let no one convince you that you are less than a God. Do not let fear imprison your spiritual growth.

11. Do not allow the unfounded belief in demons to block your communion with God.

12. The body is a living temple unto God, wherein we worship the spark of the Divine.

13. God does not create the adversities in life. By your own choice they exist to aid in your perfection.

14. Karma is nothing more than honing the wheel of evolvement. It is not retribution, but merely a balancing of experiences.

15. God allows each person the opportunity for perfection, whether you need one life or a hundred lives to reach your level of perfection.

16. Devote your life, your soul, your very existence, to the service of God. For only there will you find meaning in life.

17. War is profane; defense is compulsory.

18. Death is the act of returning Home; it should be done with grace and dignity. You may preserve that dignity by refusing prolonged use of artificial life-support systems. Let God's will be done.

19. We believe in a Mother God, Who is co-Creator with our all-loving Father God.

20. We believe that our Lord was crucified, but did not die on the cross. Instead, he went on to live his life in France with his mother and Mary Magdalene, his wife.

21. We Gnostics kept the knowledge hidden that Christ's lineage exists even today, and the truth long buried is open to research.

～～ ～～ ～～ ～～ ～～

Chapter Five

GOOD VS. EVIL

As I've stated earlier, there are religions that say that our Father is both good and bad. Yet that logic would then make God diametrically opposed to Himself, which is utter nonsense because then He wouldn't be perfect. And if that were true, why have faith's great prophets only spoken about Him with love and compassion?

I finally came to the rational conclusion that God is either all good or all bad. And the idea that He would be all bad is ludicrous because that would make Him a capricious monster Who created us to suffer.

All religions believe that God is all-knowing, loving, and merciful; yet human beings then put the "fear/guilt hooks" in . . . it's no wonder that we're so confused. However, rest assured that our perfect Father made us out of love, which doesn't play favorites. As simplistic as it seems, consider parents (at least those who genuinely love their kids)—how could they not care what their children's lives turned out to be, after they nurtured them for so many years? And if human parenting can accomplish this, imagine what God's infinite love does!

Being "Good"

We are more or less taught by our faiths that if we live a good and righteous life, we'll ascend to heaven. In his Sermon on the Mount, Jesus gave us the beatitudes of the poor in spirit, the meek, those who mourn, those who hunger and thirst after justice, the merciful, the pure of heart, the peacemakers, those who suffer persecution for justice's sake, and those who are persecuted and reviled and have evil spoken against them, untruthfully, for the sake of God. But there's nothing in this sermon that damns us or makes us feel less than Divine—after all, how could we not be Divine ourselves when that's what we come from?

The problem is that the religious leaders of humankind decided that complicated is better because the more complex something is, the more stupid the "little people" feel. Then we're told that if we ask a theological question, we can't know the answer because it's a "mystery."

I'm convinced that this issue of "doing good" is really at the core of our society's breakdown, as young people don't really have a spiritual base anywhere. So, in response, they seem to gravitate toward a hedonistic quality like the ancient Romans—they live for the moment because that's all there is. There's nothing for them to hope for, nothing to see as a reward of going to the Other Side. There's just a void inside that they try to fill up with gangs, drugs, and sex . . . a void that only God can occupy.

The suicide rate of teenagers is at an all-time high, and why not? Sometimes it doesn't seem like life is worth living. Now you might wonder about these kids' charts, but Francine has said that so many have been warned that they're coming into existence too fast or won't be prepared—and that's where humans' stubborn free-will choice employs itself.

I'm reminded here of a woman I spoke to just the other day who told me that she'd recovered memories of standing in front of the Council (a group of elders on the Other Side who help us plan our charts, along with

God, our guides, and angels), arguing with them when they warned her that she was taking on too much. She went on to attempt suicide twice in this earthly life.

This woman finally realized that she had to live by her program or do it all over again—once she did, a peace immediately came over her, and the pieces of her life fell into place. She said that when she first read one of my books she was overjoyed, because for years she thought that she was crazy. But why would she think that? Doesn't it just make logical sense that we go on a mission to learn for God and advance our souls?

When looked at as isolated incidents, it's hard to see why some individuals take on what they do in their charts, such as parenting an autistic child, contracting a rare illness, or enduring the tragic deaths of loved ones. Well, just as climbers who ascend Mt. Everest want to accomplish something that hasn't been done by very many people, we have the same thing in mind. In the small and large experiences of our lives, we write the "Everests" into our charts so that we can climb to the top and say that we did it—and we learn endurance along the way. Sure, we probably experience loneliness, depression, and even the thought of giving up, but we trudge on because it's in our soul's blueprint to do so.

It's like school, when we crammed in all our subjects and then realized how hard they were, so we either muddled through or flunked out. Yet even if we do the latter, that doesn't mean we've failed—we encounter a similar lesson again, and if we keep missing it, we just come back into another life to complete our mission or learn something new for our soul and God. And just like the person who climbs Everest, in the end, we eventually have to come back down . . . life is fleeting, and we all end up together on the Other Side.

Getting back to our charts for our all-loving God, recently I had a man tell me that he was mad at God because he'd prayed so hard to save his wife's life, but she'd died anyway. I explained that she charted to go before him so that he wouldn't be so dependent and would find the spirituality she had.

"You mean I made her go?" he asked.

"Of course not!" I replied. "This was the written contract between the two of you before you even came into life. It had nothing to do with God's not hearing your prayers—He just wouldn't interfere with your contract."

He was silent for a moment and then remarked, "Well, I *have* been searching for more answers."

I said, "That's the first step to spirituality. We all have our parts to play on the stage of life, and when the play is over, we all meet backstage and have a great party."

By discovering his spirituality, this man had the right idea. As a society, we've become so obsessed with weight, beauty, youth, money, and always being the "life of the party." Weight is a health risk, but the expression "You can never be too rich or too thin" makes me sick. How about being comfortable in our own skins? Being moderate in all things, as the Greeks say, carries a lot of truth.

Everyone and everything has a place in this world . . . but we have a habit of becoming too zealous and fanatical about things. We block out learning and become singularly focused. Having said that, each of us has to figure out what gives us passion, even if it's just being with our families or talking to God.

When spirituality fills you up, you'd be surprised at how much you don't need all the world's "trappings." But you wouldn't believe how many people I've talked to, especially in the last 10 or 15 years, who just know in their souls that this is their last time around on Earth. Others also know when they want to come back, but the majority of individuals I encounter say, "I'm done." Me, too—I'll work for God anywhere except in this hellhole.

Now when you say this, people often think that you're cynical or jaded. Well, that's not true for me—I love all of you and my family and my life, but life on Earth is so horrific these days that it gets harder and harder to stay positive. I know that's also why we see so much depression . . . and, of course, the pharmaceutical companies are making a fortune. It's not wrong to take antidepressants, but I feel that they should only be used as a last resort to survive.

I've never been against taking the medication we need, nor do I believe that we should just rely on one type of treatment; after all, God made physicians, too. I just don't think that we should run to the doctor every time we have a hard time in life. I've recommended that people who have their serotonin levels out of whack seek help, but first they should look at their lives and see if it's a medical or external problem.

For example, when I lost nine people in less than four months and then two the next year, my doctor told me that I was depressed and needed to be medicated. I replied, "You don't have a pill for grief." However, I *did* try to eat more protein to keep my blood sugar up, exercise even when I didn't want to, and work. There can be no easy way out—I just know that it will all be over someday soon, at which point I'll see my much-missed loved ones and God.

The other day, a reporter really threw me for a loop when she asked, "What hurts you, Sylvia? Is it your naysayers?"

"Heavens, no!" I exclaimed. But then after I thought about the question, I realized that my answer should have been that people think I'm rolling in money. First of all, it's simply not true, but what really hurts is that anyone could think that my motivation for writing and speaking has nothing to do with God . . . when He's always my primary focus.

Then I have to remind myself that they just don't know what phone bills, salaries, churches, and ministers cost, so I need to be human enough to hurt but rational enough to understand that people don't know what they're saying when they attack me. So I give it to God—if I rent a house and lease a van, I'm very happy (besides, I'm mobile!).

We all have our "demons" of injustice to fight, but we can't let others interfere with the charted mission that's written on our soul. I've been deceived and lost loved ones to death, and I've became discouraged many times. I've battled skepticism, lies, and injustices over and over again. I've seen the top of the success heap and the bottom of the failure pile. Yet through it all, my chart was always foremost in my mind, and that has sustained me, as has the knowledge that our Creator loves me unconditionally.

What about Evil?

Theologians have tried to explain evil for centuries. Most tended to come to the conclusion that God allows it to exist so that we can choose either "good" or "bad."

(And to diverge for a moment on the idea of hell, it was no more than a dump that burned constantly outside the city of Jerusalem. It was called "Sheol" by the ancient Israelites, which then became "Gehenna," or an abode for the wicked.)

Then we have the devil. The word *Satan* actually means "adversary," but the word became twisted to refer to the devil. (*Shaitan* is also a Muslim term for the "devil" or "Satan.")

Now, since Father and Mother God created everything, They would have made the devil, too. It may come as a surprise to some, but if you read closely, most theological texts portray the name *Lucifer* as meaning "light" and say that he was beloved by God. Francine told me that God still loves Lucifer, and even more important, understands and allows the dark entities to inhabit the world for our own enlightenment. In other words, many times we only learn from evil examples.

My mother, for example (God love her, because I couldn't), was dark, but because of her, I became a better mother. And what about those evil or dark entities? Well, in the beginning, God created everything good, but some of humankind, in their own free will, separated from God on the Other Side and went on their own way to create hate and destruction when they incarnated (which also holds up the premise that Earth is hell).

Of course our all-knowing God realized this, but things had to play out this way. For every good there is evil, and dark entities help us face adversity and come out on top. In fact, unlike what so many religions teach, God does *not* have these entities burn in hell. Instead, they'll ultimately just be absorbed back into the uncreated mass of His goodness.

People often ask me if they're dark themselves. Well, if they ask this question, they can't be. You see, dark entities don't care if they're evil, and they justify every horrendous action that they do. Good people know what right actions are, but look at Charles Manson, who had the power to make others kill for him . . . this is pure evil. Such behavior supposedly comes from God—a so-called prophet starts quoting a few scriptures, and then the masses start following. So if something doesn't feel right to you, use common sense—you're better off just loving God in your own silent way than mixing in with a band of crazy people.

Francine always says that whatever you can think of to ask can be answered in a logical way. Yet I worry that in this day and age, when people have felt that religious beliefs have failed them, they may look for a "messiah" who preaches that he is the be-all and end-all . . . that's how we get a Jim Jones or David Koresh. Just because someone has knowledge doesn't mean that he or she can rule other people's thoughts, feelings, and actions.

We hear that God loves us all equally, but then we ask ourselves how this can be when evil seems to survive without a hitch while the good suffer. Then we have God supposedly playing favorites with saints—but isn't everyone who gets to heaven a saint? Of course they are. True saints are those who raise a family, struggle to do right, and survive (and even thrive) against all odds—not just a select handful who seem to give homage to God.

Even though idols seem to be a thorn in so many religions' sides, Catholicism has statues to saints, Jesus, and the like, and I understand when they say that we're not praying to the statue but to what they represent. I defend this right to have representations because I have pictures of my grandchildren that I light candles around, and I ask the Holy Spirit to protect them. I also put a white light around all my clients, the people I love, everyone who attends my lectures, and the audiences at the *Montel* show. If I'm tired, I just ask God to put a light around the whole world.

So if our charts are set, you might wonder why I do this whole protection ritual . . . well, it neutralizes negativity. If you encounter a dark entity, you'll nullify their effect because you have your "armor" on. You can still be wounded from the battle, but not fatally (and I don't mean physically but soulwise).

We're absorbing so much these days, from wars and uprisings to illnesses and social problems, while at the same time, we're becoming more remote and isolated. When I was a girl in Kansas City, Missouri, if we heard about something on the radio—be it President Roosevelt dying, a big fire, a natural catastrophe, or what have you—we all ran out in the street and talked about it. To this day, I could tell you every person's name on both sides of Charlotte, the long street our house was on. Can any of us say this today? Maybe if you live in a small pocket in the Midwest somewhere, but most of us can't.

I don't know anyone on my street now, and I live on a cul-de-sac! Yes, I'm busy . . . and like so many who spend the whole day with people, when I go home I want peace. I'll needlepoint; watch A&E; or talk to friends, family members, or business associates on the phone; but I usually write. And through it all, I feel our Mother and Father around me. . . .

This might seem confusing, but bear with me here. God is universal, which means that He is for *everyone,* regardless of race, sexuality, or creed, and each one of us has a special relationship with Him. Our Father loves us equally, but some of us may love Him more, which just makes our souls more at peace and in a state of knowing bliss. Am I better because I love and know God? No, my free-will choice allowed me to do so. When we break down the fear, guilt, and dogma barriers, God can be our friend, our beloved, and our confidant, and the constancy of this Divine entity will never fail us. The world and its sorrow will whirl around us, but God's constancy will hold and console us.

We can't blame God for what we've chosen. When I get into those dark places of grief or pain, I say, "God, I know I chose this, but please hold my hand and help me get through it." It's like giving birth—you know that there will be pain, but to have someone there holding and coaching you makes it easier, and you hopefully give birth to a stronger, more spiritual self that shines with God's light.

Yet I know that just asking for help can be too much sometimes. I'm sure that this is why I've seen more and more people lately who are feeling more tired and depressed. We're all in such a harried and hurried society that it seems that we don't have time for anything. But we need to *make* the time to get in touch with God and help each other out—after all, the great messengers all taught that we must love God above all others, and love and support each other, too.

I've often said that after we get to this planet, we wonder what we're doing here. But the answer is always to glorify God, not only with our joys but with our trials and burdens and losses and heartaches. As we grow spiritually, we come to realize that this is a temporary plane that was made difficult so that we could hone our souls to go back to the Divine Father with knowledge. And that knowledge can be as simple as surviving this hellhole of a place called "Earth" and its continual battles between good and evil.

~ ~ ~

I'd like to end this chapter by veering off course for a bit. I've said that history is written by the winners, yet theological and religious works were all penned by men. This isn't a condemnation, but no woman's voice is ever heard giving any opinion, nor were females allowed to study—many times they couldn't even enter temples or churches without their heads covered and bowed.

Only in recent years have women such as Elaine Pagels, Barbara Thiering, and Karen Armstrong ventured into the arena. Before that, when I was studying theology—and then teaching it at Presentation High School in California—I was observed with a judicial eye. I was even asked in college (by a priest, no less) why a young woman like me wanted to study such a boring subject in a male-dominated field of endeavor. I simply replied, "Because I'm interested" and walked away.

This was the same priest who, at an assembly at the College of Saint Teresa, went into a tirade about women and how unfit they were. I remember raising my hand and asking, "Father, do you think that if it wasn't for a woman, you wouldn't be here?" I saw the dean cover her mouth, hiding a smile. (God I loved Sister Olive Louise and Sister Regina Mary, who were always on my side. And Sister Marcella Marie, my literature teacher, used to call me a rebel with a cause!) It got to the point that when I met this priest in the hall, he'd keep his head down and wouldn't talk to me. I have respect for the clergy, but I have to confess that the word *chicken* often comes to mind.

So much for my disrespectful "sins." As I've explained, the word actually means "missing the mark." This means that I might have gone off the road a bit (as we all do), but I adjusted and got back on the mark, which is what I've been ordained to do by my chart. Every single human being makes mistakes, but if we follow the Golden Rule and stay steady on our track of helping and loving, then we will become better through our efforts.

The only true wrong is the one you do with mindful vengeance and purpose to hurt without any reason. Then karma enacts that philosophy of "what goes around comes around." Now while we may have feelings of revenge toward those who have hurt us, most of us don't act on them. And there is no "sin" in the defense of loved ones or ourselves. If that were the case, we wouldn't have laws. However, the one universal law that governs us all is to love one another. I'd like to add my own codicil here: *if they are lovable*. If not, walk away and give the situation over to God.

~ ~ ~ ~ ~

Chapter Six

WHAT CAN BELIEVING IN FATHER GOD DO FOR *YOU?*

As I said earlier, there has never been a subject about which so many partial truths, half-truths, and no truths have been written than our beloved Creator (aside from Christ). Have any of the humans who are guilty of spreading such lies ever discovered the whole truth? Of course not. After all the theories and the books, one gigantic truth hangs over us, which is simpler than it appears. Every one of the great messengers just tried to show us God's work and love, but we couldn't be satisfied—rather, we had to make it complicated. It remains that there is good and evil; Earth is a training ground; and, as the poet said, God is in heaven and all is right with the world. (And if it wasn't, then the very worst thing that could happen is that we'd all go back together to our Home on the Other Side.)

When you realize that God knows we're human beings having human experiences, you come to a spiritual truth that fits so perfectly and will lead you to the road to God. Muslims, Christians, and Jews are all right—the only thing that doesn't work is the notion of a hateful, vengeful Creator Who only loves a certain group or particular individuals and sends the rest to everlasting damnation. I feel that those who believe others aren't "saved" unless they believe the way they do are in for a big surprise. To condemn others without doing anything about it is hypocritical, and as Jesus said, "Those of you who are without sin, cast the first stone."

God doesn't ever have human feelings, but if He did, could you imagine how He would look at us and wonder what's wrong with our reasoning? The one thing that I cannot stress too strongly here is our Creator's power to communicate directly with the human mind. As we begin to embrace God more, the communication becomes more real and recognizable and truly Divine. I'm not talking about those who are mentally ill and think that God tells them to kill people, for that is an aberration of the mind. No, God's voice in our soul is quiet and full of sweetness, comfort, and love.

People will say, "But what about the guides and angels, Sylvia? I talk to them, too." Well, by all means do so, as they're God's emissaries. But even though I talk to my guide Francine and my angels, for instance, never do I leave out my conversations with God the Father and writing petitions to Mother God.

≈⊚≈ ≈⊚≈ ≈⊚≈

While Catholics have saints and miracles attributed to them, when I went through my vast archives, I discovered that miracles aren't indigenous to any color, sect, creed, or sexuality. From Judaism to Islam and Zoroastrianism, every belief system has had miracles—they just haven't necessarily been publicized.

Even Novus Spiritus gets calls daily thanking our prayer line, which goes out to thousands of individuals at nine o'clock every night, for miraculous cures and changes in lives. I once asked people to write in to my Website about any angel encounters they might have experienced. Almost two-thirds of the responses detailed cures, miraculous escapes from catastrophes, accidents averted, and so on. Of course God sends angels, so who's to say that the individuals who thought they were talking to their spirit guides or angels weren't in fact communicating with Him?

Why can't we believe that our Divine Parents or Jesus could, in fact, visit us? Is it the feeling of unworthiness that has been drummed into humankind, which says that we're too lowly to see the Divine? That's like having a caretaker who loves us unconditionally, but we can't see or ever hear from him! How illogical is that? Forget faith . . . let's employ our intellect and rationale here.

I've personally had miracles in my life that can't be explained. For example, I should have died at the age of 26 with an acute illness, and I should have been killed in an accident years later . . . was it not God's intervention that saved me?

ళొ ళొ ళొ

The other thing that bears repeating here is that the more you lean toward and love your Creator, the more psychic you'll become. All gifts come from God, especially when you're a tube of knowledge and healing. You do give up your will to our Father and others, but trust me on this one—no matter how dark it gets, He finds you with a large flashlight. He is really telling you not to be afraid of the dark, for He will always be there, and soon you'll be back Home—safe, happy, and proud that you made it through.

When I was on a late-night talk show once, I had a female Wiccan call in and ask me if I believed in them. "Of course I do," I said. "You have a great devotion to Mother God, and since you're a white [positive-energy] Wiccan, you are a nature lover and cause no harm to any living creature."

I don't believe in the dark side of any religion, even Christianity, since humankind has a tendency to take what's good and sometimes mold it into something negative. But that's not because of God—that's letting vanity overtake people. Or some become their own deities and can't see outside of themselves. Loving ourselves is a cardinal rule, but not to the extent that we forsake all others and our Divine moral principles.

Christ said, "Be ye therefore perfect, even as your Father which is in heaven is perfect" (Matthew 5:48). So, again, we can be as perfect in our souls as God is— even if we make mistakes in our human bodies, which exist in a world designed to give us many temptations. The flesh is weak, and God knows this, but if the soul is strong, it clings and cleaves to Him.

As I've said many times, faith is exhausting, while knowledge is comforting and brings you peace. When you know something to be true, you don't have the anxiety about whether you're right or wrong; consequently, you don't have to convince people to quell your own doubts. When you believe in our beloved Father, you don't have any doubts. You're left in the peace of knowing, and you can search for more truth and utilize your findings to help others. You also realize that the truth will eventually reach those who are searching for it . . . it's only a matter of time.

~~ ~~ ~~ ~~ ~~

Chapter Seven

FREQUENTLY
ASKED QUESTIONS

D oing 20 readings a day (when I can) is something I enjoy almost as much as I do lecturing and writing. Over the years clients have told me that through my books, they've found peace and a loving relationship with God that they never had before. They even thank me for being brave enough to put my words out there. This surprises me more than anything—it truly doesn't take bravery to tell what you feel and know is true.

Since I'm asked countless questions about God and spirituality, I thought that it would be nice to include my answers to the most frequently asked queries from people just like you.

Q. Why do we pick our particular charts?

A. Because when we're on the Other Side, we feel so good that we decide (along with God, our guides, and the angels) that we can do it. Then we get down here to Earth and change our minds because it's so tough. But we also have the knowledge that this life is transient and that it's for our soul's ascension to get through it.

Q. I've done some bad things in my life. How can God forgive me?

A. Our Father is perfect and omnipotent, so He knows your life and your shortcomings. Even Jesus said that the best of men fall seven times a day. God forgives you constantly, for His love is unconditional, but you also have to forgive *yourself.*

Don't do anything to hurt yourself or anyone else. We are all human and feel pain, but hopefully we get to a point that we realize we're only hurting our temple that houses God. So protect and forgive yourself. Shield yourself from doing the same things over again, and realize that you probably didn't do anything with a malicious motive. It's like the original Gnostic teachings say—know your "True Self."

Q. How do I know if I'm on track?

A. If you ask, you are! Only good people care if they're on track—dark entities don't. They feel that they're never wrong, that everything is someone else's fault and never theirs, for they are the true sociopaths of the world.

Q. How do I know that my loved ones made it Home?

A. The percentage of people who make it to the Other Side is about 99.9 percent. There's a very small percentage that become ghosts, but even they eventually make it Home. In our earthly time, it may seem like it takes a while, but in their void of time, they're not suffering as much as you think. Most of the time they're upset that someone's occupying "their" space. But God eventually helps them—with the aid of their loved ones and guide— and brings them back Home.

Q. Is there such a thing as the devil?

A. There is a group of dark entities that seem to

be led by one entity. You can call him Satan, Lucifer, the devil, or whatever, but he doesn't run around in a red suit with pitchfork and horns. And like any other dark soul, he doesn't actually exert very much power.

You see, dark entities can't really hurt your soul, but they *can* test you, tempt you, mentally torture you, physically abuse you, drain you, and make you depressed. They really want to render you impotent so that you despair, and that's the real enemy of spirituality. But they can't curse you or ever possess you because you're self-contained as a temple from God.

The more we dwell in darkness and desperation, the more these emotions feed on themselves, and the light of God is blocked from getting in. Yet it's so easy to just ask for God's light to come in, for the Christ consciousness to surround us, and for our angels to protect us—believe me, the darkness will leave.

Q. Can God speak to us? Does He or She even have a voice?

A. Yes to both. It's interesting how the TV show *Joan of Arcadia* showed God being able to take any form and talk to this young girl. The movie *Oh, God!*

with George Burns was very entertaining, too, and it made a lot of good points about Him. But sometimes it's hard to discern whether messages are coming from a guide or God, even though both come from the same source. Nevertheless, when I'm writing or lecturing about our Creator, I get an almost euphoric feeling; while many times after I've been on *Montel* or writing, lecturing, or doing a reading, a different feeling comes over me. I'll read what I've written or lectured on and know that it was good, but it wasn't me. I'll say to myself, *Wow! Where did that come from?* and then of course I know that it's from God, not Sylvia.

Stop and think about how many times a friend has asked you a question and you open your mouth to hear this wonderful knowledge pouring out that you weren't even thinking of. Well, that's God!

Q. Do we see Father God on the Other Side?

A. People who have had near-death experiences claim that they've seen this magnificent Being of light Who is beyond description. Unlike Mother God, Who can stand in front of you with defined lines and a voluptuous figure for as long as She wants, God also can take shape but is somewhat blurred. He chooses not to hold his form for very long because His energy is so great. Francine says that on the Other Side, they see Mother God frequently, but our Father only comes out in form once in a while for a short period. But the best part is that every cell of our being on the Other Side resonates with the sense of God. How glorious that must be—no wonder we cry when we're born into life!

Q. Why does the Old Testament give us a different view of God than the New Testament does?

A. The reason for this was because Moses and most of the early scrolls were in rebuttal to the gods of Babylon, Greece, and especially Egypt. The only way to make your deity more powerful and attract more followers is to report that He only loves the ones that He chooses, and all others are condemned. This, of course, keeps people in line, but it tragically has seeped into religions that still exist today. "The fear of God," "God is angry," and "God is vengeful and jealous" are concerns that have stemmed from a humanized spiteful God Who sometimes seems to be insane. He loves us, then He doesn't; He favors us, then we fall out of His favor. No wonder humankind never knows whether we're on or off track and if God could condemn us to hell on a whim.

Q. How should I pray to God?

A. I like this one: "Dear Father, this day is for You. Help me to do Your will and live and help people today. Amen."

Prayer is good because it brings us closer to God, but doesn't affect Him because He is already in a state of loving us. I'm constantly amazed that people don't understand that our Father always knows our actions and thoughts. Sure, I pray at night, but I can't spend my life in supplication. Neither did Buddha, Mohammed, or Christ—they were all too busy teaching, healing, and helping.

Life can (and should) be an active prayer for God, while to sit for hours with our eyes closed and hands folded has always seemed so passively selfish to me. Why not go out and do good and magnify the God within us? As I tell my ministers, "If you haven't counseled someone on the phone today, seen a sick person, or even smiled at someone sad, then it's a lost day that you can't recover."

To wrap up here, I thought I'd tell you this story. As I was writing earlier, I thought, *Well, besides writing, what did you do today, Sylvia?* Just then the bell on my hotel door rang, and the maid came in. I moved outside so as not to bother her. Then she came outside to clean, and as I passed her I felt that she was down.

So I asked, "How are you today?"

She answered, "Okay, I guess," which, of course, meant that she wasn't.

I looked at her and said, "Your son will come home from the war."

Her face lit up, and she replied, "Oh, thank you, Miss Sylvia!"

Now not all of you are psychic, but how about a smile or a tip of a few extra dollars to show people that you appreciate them, or at least a thank-you for the nice job they did? How often we fail (and I'm including myself here) to honor those who give us service to make our lives easier. When I hear people say, "Well, it's their job, and they get paid for it . . . why should I thank them?" I visualize a whole plate of spaghetti on their heads. And that makes me feel a whole lot better.

∿∿ ∿∿ ∿∿ ∿∿ ∿∿

Afterword

I've found that as soon as I feel that I can know something even fairly well, a whole new area opens up, but it's such a joy to always be exploring and gathering more information. I don't know about you, but it makes my heart sing!

I was talking to my office staff this morning (because I'm currently on the road), and my secretary and I were musing about all the petty gripes we've all gone through over the years, but how we've all stuck together through thick and thin. After kicking it around for a while, we decided that the reason we were still with one another was thanks to a combination of the spiritual quest, our love of Mother and Father God, and our attempts to live by Christ's teachings in the best way we could.

It's like that old saying of putting the carrot in front of the donkey—we're trying to strive for a greater good, and that goal has kept us together . . . most of us more than 30 years. I often think that if marriages had the same objective, there wouldn't be any divorce.

Many of my staff have seen me through my own divorces, a bankruptcy 20 years ago, the deaths of loved ones, and financial problems with the IRS (because of a marriage gone sideways). I've seen them through their own financial difficulties, tragedies, and problems with their families. Through it all, we've hung together. Pam, who's been with me for 32 years, remembers when we were so bad off that we used to have potlucks so that we could eat.

I'm not trying to elicit sympathy here—I just want to illustrate that through all the troubles, depression, illnesses, and the like, my staff and I have clung to our belief in an afterlife that's as real to us as anything in this life. My 100 ministers, hundreds of study groups that call for a spiritual shot in the arm, and a staff of 26 in offices in Campbell, California; Seattle; and Los Angeles; give each other hope and know that if one of us falls, many will be there to pick us up.

That is really what God is about. He isn't condemning or judgmental, but He is always there. Whenever I've gone to Kenya, I've often thought that they really have the right idea. They thank God for the good that day and give homage to Him even if things haven't gone "right." Aside from the fact that they still fear the God of nature (drought may mean that He is angry, for instance), there it's understandable, for they have no other explanation for how fickle nature can be. The Masai live for the day, which is why if one is put in jail, he'll die—his "now" is forever. This is the tough side of it, but on the upside is the fact that today is the rest of the Masai's life, and he doesn't think about tomorrow. So if he only has 30 pence to his name but can dance the night away to honor God, everything's okay. The tribe typifies living for the day—or the moment—and I truly envy that.

∂ℓ ∂ℓ ∂ℓ

I've found that the more I talk to people about their future, especially as they become increasingly spiritual and feel God's unconditional love, the more intuitive they become. I'll say something to them and get a response like, "Sylvia, that's so strange . . . I already started to do that," or "I was thinking about that person just the other day." We psychics can't see it all, as that would take away from our own learning process. One small example of this came on the day that I nicked my foot while running up the steps with bags full of groceries. The next day it was swollen, and after seeing the doctor, I found out that I had blood poisoning from the moss on the steps.

I came home and was rather aggravated that I had to sit on the couch with my foot in hot water and take antibiotics (which don't sit well with me anyway). Out of frustration, I asked Francine, "What in the heck is this about?"

Very quietly, yet distinctly, these words came back: "Just maybe you're running too fast and should slow down."

"Couldn't you have just told me?" I retorted.

"Would you have listened?" came the soft answer. Damn, I hate it when she's right!

Now for a more tragic scenario, when my beloved dad was dying, I was standing there torn. I wanted him to stay, but not like that—I didn't want him to suffer. He could always read my mind, and right then he looked up at me and said, "Don't you know that I can do more for you now on the Other Side than I can here anymore?"

After the pain of his loss receded somewhat, I realized that when times get bad, he's there for me . . . as all our loved ones are on the Other Side.

◈◈ ◈◈ ◈◈

Imagine the following scenario:

You're driving down the highway when off to the side you see a dirt road. Feeling adventurous, you decide to follow it. You drive on the winding path, kicking up dust, but there in the distance you see what looks like a small cabin. As you get closer, you see a cross on the small peaked roof. You realize that this must be an old chapel or perhaps a place that a family put on their property to go and worship.

You approach the door, and with just a slight push, it swings open. All of a sudden this tiny place seems to expand, as if the walls collapsed or grew higher and longer. There is an altar, but no adornment. You walk closer, and then you see this beautiful Entity standing with arms outstretched. There seems to be light coming from every finger. The face is chiseled with soft eyes, and the hair is wavy. The Being is dressed in robes that emanate a vibrant gold and purple. Around Him, angels are standing and sitting in front, behind, on the sides, and as far back as you can see . . . all phylums, with all colors of wings. Some are singing, but all seem to be centered around this gorgeous Being of light, and the overwhelming love you feel transports your soul beyond anything you have ever known before.

Wouldn't that be the greatest situation if you could actually do this and feel the true sense of God? Well, why can't you? Just because someone told you that you couldn't? Look inside your soul for your own chapel, where Father God in all His glory is watching and loving you.

Keep searching and studying, and one day you'll know the logical truth of what so many tried to bring to us, but were thwarted by greed and power and money.

God love you. I do. . . .
Sylvia

~~ ~~ ~~ ~~ ~~

Thank you, God, for all the joy
You have given me through
my family, friends,
the readers of my books,
my clients, and staff.

— **Sylvia**

ABOUT THE AUTHOR

Sylvia Browne is the #1 *New York Times* best-selling author and world-famous psychic medium who appears regularly on *The Montel Williams Show* and *Larry King Live,* as well as making countless other media and public appearances. With her down-to-earth personality and great sense of humor, Sylvia thrills audiences on her lecture tours and still has time to write numerous immensely popular books. She has a master's degree in English literature and plans to write as long as she can hold a pen.

Sylvia is the president of the Sylvia Browne Corporation; and is the founder of her church, the Society of Novus Spiritus, located in Campbell, California. Please contact her at: **www.sylvia.org,** or call **(408) 379-7070** for further information about her work.

∿∿ ∿∿ ∿∿ ∿∿ ∿∿

NOTES